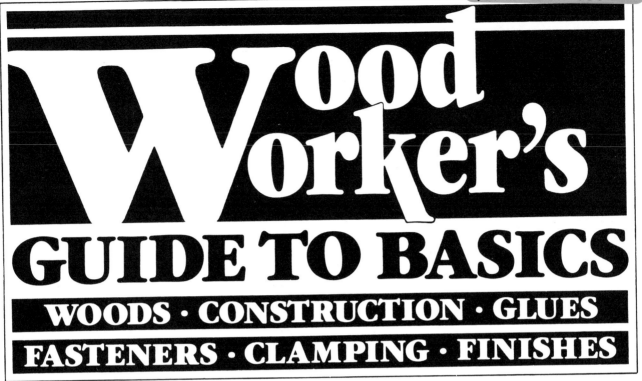

Wood Worker's GUIDE TO BASICS

WOODS · CONSTRUCTION · GLUES
FASTENERS · CLAMPING · FINISHES

R.J. DeChristoforo

George Daniels

Jackson Hand

POPULAR SCIENCE BOOKS

NEW YORK

CONTENTS

Cover photograph courtesy of Garret Wade Company

Copyright © 1984 by Times Mirror Magazine, Inc.

Published by
Popular Science Books
Times Mirror Magazines, Inc.
380 Madison Avenue
New York, NY 10017

ISBN 0-943822-29-7

Second Printing, 1985

Manufactured in the United States of America

FURNITURE WOODS

The finishing qualities of the wood you use in your woodworking project depend on whether the wood is "open-grained" or "close-grained." The strength of the finished piece depends on the type of wood you choose—hardwood or softwood, straight-grained or knotted—how the wood was cut from the tree, and how you use it in constructing the piece. A basic knowledge of the characteristics of those woods commonly available to the home craftsman, with an eye toward selecting the one with qualities best suited to the piece, is essential for the successful completion of every project.

Mahogany. This is a red-brown wood of medium density and hardness, with open pores, even texture and sometimes striking grain patterns. Its woodworking qualities and finished appearance vary with country of origin: Honduras and African varieties are generally best; Philippine (lauan) is often low grade. Widely available in lumber form and veneers, it can become even more mellow and beautiful with age, is fine for carving, resists warping and works easily with machine or hand tools.

Maple. Hard maple is strong, hard, and dense, and despite the fact that it can dull tools faster than many other woods, is very popular with home-craftsmen and commercial furniture makers. Two popular grain patterns are curly maple and bird's-eye. It's an excellent wood for turning and takes a beautiful, smooth finish. Its durability is attested to by its use in bowling-alley lanes and for other equally demanding purposes.

Soft maple is easier to work but lacks the strength of the hard maple. It will machine well and takes a good finish. It may contain some red or brown streaks but you can use these to advantage by creating unusual and interesting effects. You'll find it used today in the reproduction of antiques and, also, in the construction of modern pieces.

Birch. The wood of the birch tree comes close to being maple's twin. It too is hard and close-grained but its heartwood is red. It's strong and straight and excellent for use in rails, doors, and work-table tops. It's a good wood for turning and is not difficult to finish. Quite often it is finished in walnut or mahogany, but mostly you'll see it finished similarly to maple or left blond and natural.

Cherry. A peculiar characteristic of cherry is that it turns cherry-red when exposed to sunlight. Antique collectors are apt to judge the age of cherry furniture by its color. Few woods endure the ravages of time and use more gracefully. The pattern of its grain is similar to maple but less pronounced. It's close-grained and pleasant to work with, strong, does not warp easily and makes a good glue joint. It is not as easy to find these days as some of the other popular cabinet and furniture woods, but it's worth searching out.

Gum. Gum is on the list of important hardwoods and is usually designated as being *sap gum* or *red gum*. The heartwood is the darker while wood taken from the outer circumference of the trunk (the sap wood) is lighter and softer and, generally, not as desirable as the red heartwood. Both, however, are often used to simulate mahogany or walnut. Gum has a tendency to warp so is seldom used as wide boards, but it glues easily, sands well and isn't bad for lathe turning.

Oak. Red oak and white oak cover over 250 species. The white is preferred since it has a finer texture for furniture work, is harder and more durable. It's definitely "open-grain" so is tougher to finish than some other woods. Oak of any species is really tough wood, a fact appreciated by craftsmen of yesteryears who used it to make oxen yokes, wagon wheels, tongues, and wagon frames; and you've probably seen "golden oak" sideboards and dining room sets.

The particular terrain where the tree grows makes a difference in the quality of the wood. If it's hillgrown it is easier to work and better for furniture. The stringy fiber of the lowlands oak is more useful for truck bodies, tool handles, and similar items. Oak isn't used too often in wide boards since it has a tendency to warp. You'll find it used quite often today in stair treads, interior trim, flooring, thresholds, etc.

Poplar. Poplar is a versatile wood. Turn it, shape it, machine it, paint it, stain it, treat it to resemble walnut or mahogany—and it has the blessed quality of resisting warpage. It has a minimum of grain and its color runs from gray to yellow so it's not very attractive or interesting when finished naturally, but many craftsmen do prefer it to pine for painted furniture and trim.

Walnut. Walnut is a proud product of American forests and one of the finest cabinet and furniture woods available. But it's not limited to domestic growth; Britain, France, China, and other countries have it and in some of these places it is valued for its fruit alone.

Walnut has pleasing grain variations and possesses an inherent beauty that should be emphasized with a natural finish. A good oil finish does it justice but a good oil finish is never really completed. An old craftsman used to say, "First soak the wood in warm linseed oil. When the wood will absorb no more, wipe off the excess with a clean, lint-free cloth and set the work aside for a few days. Then repeat the process—daily for a week; weekly for a month; monthly for a year; and yearly thereafter."

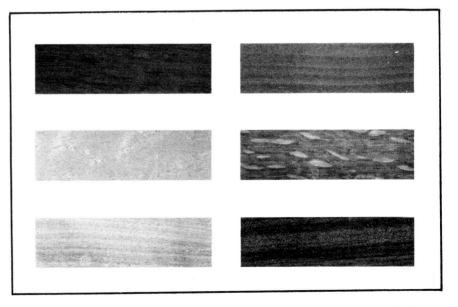

Samples of most popular woods used by home craftsmen show the different grain and color characteristics of each species. Counterclockwise from top left are: mahogany, "bird's eye" maple, birch, walnut, oak (with highlighted grain pattern or "flakes" produced by quarter-sawing), and cherry.

Walnut never stops becoming more and more beautiful with each oil application, and if you are a real craftsman of the old pot-bellied stove days you won't stoop to use a cloth but will find serene joy in rubbing the oil into the wood with the palms of your hands. Art objects made from walnut are often totally submerged in oil for a period of time, then removed and hand polished.

Basswood. Basswood is the softest of the hardwoods. You've seen it used for drawing boards and for mouldings; and if you are a jigsaw enthusiast, you've used it for fretwork. American sources of basswood are the linden and tulip tree. It's easy to work and carve and doesn't warp easily. Grain is very slight and often nonexistent, so it's a good wood for craftwork like wood-burning. It sands well, makes a good, strong glue-joint. Its characteristics make it particularly suitable as a core stock for panels. Finishing, however, is not too simple and a non-grain-raising stain is recommended. If you should seek a natural finish, be sure to use a sanding sealer first.

Pine. California pine, ponderosa pine, sugar pine, Idaho pine, northern white, fat pine—the chances are, if you buy it in quantity, you're apt to find examples of many species in the one lot of lumber. It's usually soft-textured and easy to work with machines or by hand. You can buy it clear or knotty;

it's adaptable and can be finished in various ways. Too many people, however, try to make it look like maple. Commercial stains, often sold under names like knotty pine, honey pine, antique, driftwood, etc., are available and will produce a much more attractive finish on pine than trying to make it resemble maple or walnut or mahogany or anything else but pine. Of course, some of the better pines are excellent for any project that requires painting.

Rare and fancy woods. There are many other woods—some used extensively, some rarely, some so scarce they must be veneered to make them more available, some so weak they must be reinforced with plywood in order to display their intricate and delicate grain patterns.

There is fir, redwood, cypress, spruce, hemlock, ash, willow, chestnut, beech, larch and elm. The "ironwoods"—teak and ebony and hickory. The exotics—rosewood, zebra-wood, korina, gaboon, lauan, snakewood, prima vera, and on and on.

One good way to get a look at some common and rare woods is to acquire a set of samples. Sets of this type are available from wood supply and craftsman supply houses that do business by mail.

Innovations and variations. Burls, butts, crotches, produce particular formations which affect the grain pattern. Curly

figures in the wood are produced by fiber distortions and are the result of depressions in growth rings, filled in or compensated for by succeeding growth. More about this in the section on plywood.

Different methods of sawing through logs produce different markings; not that the sawing itself contributes anything beyond texture but that the different cuts reveal various aspects of the grain pattern.

Plain-sliced or flat-cuts are made, cut after cut, straight through the log. Quarter-sawing is done by cutting at right angles to the tree growth-rings. Rift-sawing is done at an angle to the growth-rings of 45 degrees. The common, plain stripe is derived by cutting on the quarter, which means slicing a log into four, wedge-shaped pieces and then cutting from one of the flat sides of each wedge.

Lumber is measured and the price figured by a unit called the "board foot," based on the actual size of the lumber in its rough-sawed state. A board foot is simply a piece of wood which measures 1″ by 12″ by 12″ or any equivalent. A piece of lumber 2″ by 6″ by 12″ is also a board foot. A piece 2″ by 12″ by 12″ is *two* board feet.

Shaped pieces such as mouldings are sold by the lineal or running foot, and prices are affected by the size and the elaborateness of the design and/or the material. Laths, and shingles and shakes too, are sold by the bun-

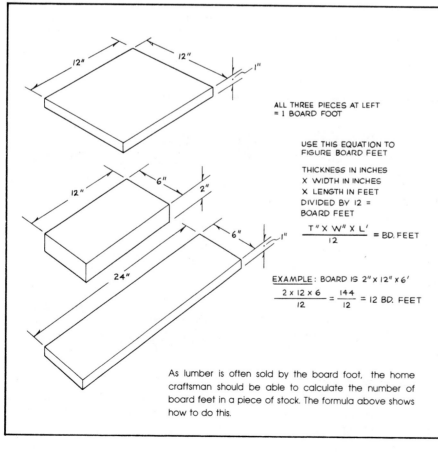

ALL THREE PIECES AT LEFT = 1 BOARD FOOT

USE THIS EQUATION TO FIGURE BOARD FEET

THICKNESS IN INCHES
X WIDTH IN INCHES
X LENGTH IN FEET
DIVIDED BY 12 =
BOARD FEET

$$\frac{T'' \times W'' \times L'}{12} = BD. \ FEET$$

EXAMPLE: BOARD IS 2″ x 12″ x 6′
$$\frac{2 \times 12 \times 6}{12} = \frac{144}{12} = 12 \ BD. \ FEET$$

As lumber is often sold by the board foot, the home craftsman should be able to calculate the number of board feet in a piece of stock. The formula above shows how to do this.

NOMINAL AND ACTUAL SIZES OF LUMBER

Nominal Size	Actual Size
1 x 2	$^{25}/_{32}$″ x 1⅝″
2 x 2	1⅝ x 1⅝
1 x 3	$^{25}/_{32}$ x 2⅝
2 x 3	1⅝ x 2⅝
1 x 4	$^{25}/_{32}$ x 3⅝
2 x 4	1⅝ x 3⅝
1 x 5	$^{25}/_{32}$ x 4⅝
1 x 6	$^{25}/_{32}$ x 5⅝
2 x 6	1⅝ x 5⅝
1 x 8	$^{25}/_{32}$ x 7½
2 x 8	1⅝ x 7½
1 x 10	$^{25}/_{32}$ x 9½
2 x 10	1⅝ x 9½
1 x 12	$^{25}/_{32}$ x 11½
2 x 12	1⅝ x 11½

dle or ''square''; plywood by the square foot. If you ask your dealer for the price of ¼" or ¾" plywood—or any available thickness for that matter—and he tells you ''so much per foot,'' you don't have to worry about thickness since each thickness has its own price-per-foot.

Lumber yards stock lumber in standard sizes, usually starting at 8' long and increasing by two-foot jumps up to 20' or 24'. If your requirements call for a piece 1" by 12" by 7', you can get it cut to that length, but you will probably pay for the 1' that is cut off, unless the man explains to you that his shortest stock is 8' long and suggests that you take the whole 8' and saw it to length yourself so you can save the cut-off.

It's wise to buy lumber in the lowest grade suitable for your purpose. Let the project, or the project component decide. It doesn't make sense to use a beautiful clear pine for storage shelves in the garage when ordinary shelving will do.

Many times, a good material in a lower grade will do for even a ''good'' project, especially if you don't need too much of it. This is accomplished by culling the lower grade—that is, sawing it up into pieces as big as possible or to the dimensions required, but planning the cuts so the blemishes will be discarded. Lumber can even be salvaged from crates if the project permits use of such material. Many a box or crate originally built to hold apples or oranges has been reclaimed by a practical craftsman, carefully taken apart, and made into an attractive project.

PLYWOOD

The use of plywood, even in fine-furniture construction, has many advantages:

1. The construction of the panel itself provides great strength plus resistance to warping and cracking.
2. The manufacturing techniques make available large panels which eliminate the need to glue up boards to make a wide piece of stock.
3. It permits the use of rare or beautiful woods which might otherwise be unavailable or prohibitively costly.
4. It can even improve on nature since the grain patterns and figures of the surface veneers can be arranged and matched for attractive effects. Blemishes and imperfections can be removed before the veneer is applied.
5. A beautiful wood which may lack the qualities needed for strong construction can still be available through its use as a plywood veneer.

Generally speaking, there is ''softwood'' plywood and ''hardwood'' plywood. These may be arbitrary designations at this point, but most plywood manufactured for construction and industrial use utilizes Douglas fir or one of twenty-three other Western softwoods. Douglas fir is the most prominent.

Hardwood plywood generally refers to plywood which has all its plies made of hardwood or just the face veneer. You can get it as ''all-veneer,'' which, as the name implies, is construction entirely of veneers. It may be a ''lumber-core'' plywood, which is mostly five-ply and has a thick center-piece of solid wood. This type is usually made as a five-ply panel. Composite panels—specialty plywood—may have a core of some wood-base material such as flakeboard or particleboard with visible outer veneers of hardwood.

Wise utilization of plywood calls for some preplanning so cuts can be made with a minimum of waste and so grain direction on various components will be compatible when the project is viewed as a whole. This may be accomplished by following the main-part system described in a previous chapter of project making—planning the grain direction and cutting out the main parts first and then going on from there—or a scale plan of the panel can be penciled on paper and the parts of the project scaled onto that. This may not be too important when a utility-grade plywood is used for a painted project, but when you buy a panel of fancy hardwood that you plan to use for a natural-finish project, it can be quite critical.

The term *veneering,* as related to plywood, applies to the process of bonding a thin layer of decorative wood to the surface of a thicker piece, usually less attractive. The object in veneering is not merely to disguise inexpensive wood as a costlier wood. Often, veneering is the only practical means of combining exotic appearance with adequate strength. The reason: Many of the most highly prized grain patterns are found only in the

Interior Type

Use these terms when you specify plywood	Description and Most Common Uses	Veneer Grade			Most Common Thickness (inch)				
		Face	Back	Inner Plies					
N-N, N-A N-B INT-APA	Cabinet quality. For natural finish furniture, cabinet doors, built-ins, etc. Special order items.	N	N.A. or B	C					¾
N-D INT-APA	For natural finish paneling. Special order item.	N	D	D	¼				
A-A INT-APA	For applications with both sides on view. Built-ins, cabinets, furniture and partitions. Smooth face; suitable for painting.	A	A	D	¼	⅜	½	⅝	¾
A-B INT-APA	Use where appearance of one side is less important but two smooth solid surfaces are necessary.	A	B	D	¼	⅜	½	⅝	¾
A-D INT-APA	Use where appearance of only one side is important. Paneling, built-ins, shelving, partitions, and flow racks.	A	D	D	¼	⅜	½	⅝	¾
B-B INT-APA	Utility panel with two smooth sides. Permits circular plugs.	B	B	D	¼	⅜	½	⅝	¾
B-D INT-APA	Utility panel with one smooth side. Good for backing, sides of built-ins. Industry: shelving, slip sheets, separator boards and bins.	B	D	D	¼	⅜	½	⅝	¾
DECORATIVE PANELS INT-APA	Rough sawn, brushed, grooved, or striated faces. For paneling, interior accent walls, built-ins, counter facing, displays, and exhibits.	C or btr.	D	D	5/16	⅜	½	⅝	
PLYRON INT-APA	Hardboard face on both sides. For counter tops, shelving, cabinet doors, flooring. Faces tempered, tempered, smooth, or screened.	C & D			½	⅝	¾		

Courtesy American Plywood Assoc.

weakest part of the tree. The burl grains of walnut, poplar, and other species actually develop in excrescences of the trunk caused by an injury to the tree. Yet the veneers cut from these burls contain decorative figuring sought for top-quality cabinetwork. Because of the curled and wavy grain, however, wood of this type does not have the strength required for structural parts. So wood for the basic structural part is selected for strength rather than appearance, and veneer is bonded to it for its decorative value.

Weight, too, is sometimes a factor in the decision to use a veneer. Tropical woods such as ebony, with a weight close to 80 pounds per cubic foot, might easily make a large piece of furniture too heavy to handle if used in solid form. So lighter woods are used for the underlying structure.

Methods of veneering. The traditional veneering method calls for clamping the veneer tightly to the glue-coated surface to be veneered. For large areas, a veneer press is widely used. You can save money by making your own veneer press, using ready-made press screws. Small veneering jobs, however, can be done with ordinary C-clamps or handscrews and scraps of plywood.

Veneering makes it possible to extend the availability of those variations in tree formations which result in distinctive and beautiful grain patterns. For example, a board foot of bird's-eye maple won't go very far, but if it were sliced into veneer, it would cover a good-sized panel. The following is a brief discussion of other figures and patterns that are available in veneers.

Burls. The result of an injury to the growing, outer layer of certain tree cells creates a need for a protective covering in that area and causes an abnormality of growth that produces wood in knurled, uneven formations. These large, wart-like growths are cut from the tree and peeled like an apple to produce a valuable and attractive veneer.

The herringbone veneer pattern is formed by cutting straight-grained veneer into strips angled to the grain, and flipping them in alternate strips.

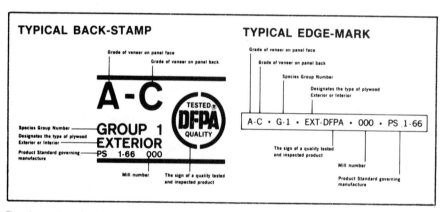

TYPICAL BACK-STAMP

Grade of veneer on panel face
Grade of veneer on panel back

A-C

GROUP 1 EXTERIOR
PS 1-66 000

Species Group Number
Designates the type of plywood
Exterior or Interior
Product Standard governing manufacture

TESTED DFPA QUALITY

Mill number
The sign of a quality tested and inspected product

TYPICAL EDGE-MARK

Grade of veneer on panel face
Grade of veneer on panel back
Species Group Number
Designates the type of plywood
Exterior or Interior

A-C • G-1 • EXT-DFPA • 000 • PS 1-66

The sign of a quality tested and inspected product
Mill number
Product Standard governing manufacture

The plywood grade stamps with symbols described. The grade stamp on the back or edge of plywood is your assurance of quality. Look for it and be wary of panels without it. (American Plywood Assn.)

This matched diamond pattern is angle-cut from straight-grain veneer. As a guide in veneer cutting and matching, draw lines on paper, approximating grain type. Then cut the paper with scissors and make experimental matching patterns. Finally, cut the veneer with a fine-toothed saw and joint the edges.

In the left-hand photo, tape holds together diamond-matched veneer along juncture lines. The pattern is formed by joining identical veneers cut from the same "flitch." This is a squared timber cut from the original log. You can buy veneer already matched, as shown, or make your own, using identically grained veneers. In the right-hand photo, the tape has been removed to show the matched-grain pattern. Many other patterns are possible, as shown in the drawings that follow.

By cutting both across and with the grain of the veneer you can produce four-piece matching like this. Make the kerf (cutting line) as narrow as possible by using a thin-bladed saw.

Butts. Some sudden growth of a tree can cause the wood fibers in its base to compress, wrinkle, and twist. This writhing movement of growth traces intricate figures from which veneers can be made. "Butts" are the stumps of such trees, cross-sections of which are sliced to produce the figure. You don't get this in all wood, but of those in which it is found, walnut is the most common.

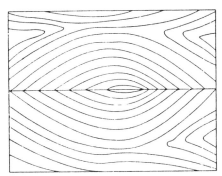

Where grain pattern permits, end-to-end matching gives an interesting appearance like this. But not all grain patterns lend themselves to this treatment. Examine the grain and decide.

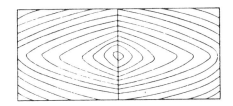

Side-to-side matching is easy when you have veneers from the same flitch. Check with your supplier as to the availability of suitable veneers. Also check on the availability of veneers already matched and taped in the pattern you want .

Crotch. Where a main branch leaves the trunk of the tree or where the trunk itself separates to form a fork, that's where you'll get a beautiful veneer. It's possible to imagine the twisting and wrinkling that must take place at those points to adjust to such a separation in the growth of its parts. There is also "feather crotch," which has a feather-like figure from being cut near the heart of the log; and "moon crotch," which is a result of cutting near the bark.

Some other figures and patterns are known as fiddleback, leaf, flake, blisterswirl, mottle, etc.

In addition to the design inherent in the wood itself, the method of cutting the log affects the results. Straight and quarter-sawing is seen a good deal on oak where it reveals a flake pattern. Some very hard woods which are difficult to slice may also be treated in this fashion. Ebony is an example. Rift-cutting is where the knife operates at a 45-degree angle to the rings and produces a striped effect. A back-cut is the result of a procedure that allows the heart wood to be sliced first. Half-rounding is done to yield sheets which will have a symmetrical pattern when veneered. A striped effect is produced when the log is quartered and cut at approximate right angles to the growth rings. The rotary cut peels ribbons of veneer from a lathe-mounted log.

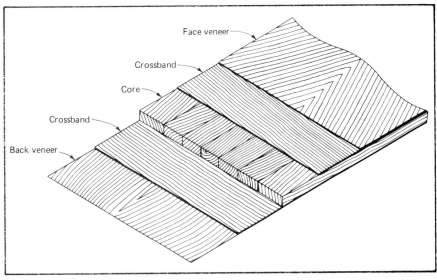

If you make the complete assembly for a large, veneered panel such as a tabletop, layering should be like this. Note the narrow core strips edge-glued with grain of alternate strips reversed. Crossbands at right angles to the core bond it tightly and minimize distortion. Back veneer runs parallel to the face veneer.

COMPOSITION BOARD

HARDBOARD

Hardboard is made from wood chips which are reduced to the basic wood fibers. Then these are re-united under heat and pressure to form a panel product which is grainless, dense, and durable, and which is adaptable to many uses. There are no knots or other imperfections.

Since it is grainless, its strength runs in either direction and it can be easily worked with the same tools you use on natural lumber. It will, however, dull tools faster since it is harder and more abrasive.

Hardboard, manufactured as described and made available without additional treatment, is *standard* hardboard, widely used in construction and in the fabrication of various products. Other processes result in hard-

board with particular properties, such as *tempered* hardboard which, because of additional treatment and heat-treating of the standard product, takes on added hardness, stiffness, strength, and more resistance to abrasion and moisture.

You can get hardboard with one smooth side (SIS) or two smooth sides (S2S) and with a good variety of surface textures such as *striated, grooved, tiled,* and *embossed.* You're probably familiar with it in its *perforated* form. It is also available prefinished, prime-coated and in wood-grain patterns. Panel sizes range up to 5' in width and up to 16' in length; thickness can run from ⅛" up to ¾". It has found great use as a core over which are bonded beautiful veneers, fabrics, plastics, and other materials.

In home-workshop furniture construction it is used in case backs, vertical dividers and drawer bottoms, or as a cover material such as a "disposable" workbench top.

Popular thicknesses stocked by most dealers include ⅛", ³⁄₁₆", and ¼" in both standard and tempered varieties. If you need it for indoor use, ask for the standard; for outdoor use or indoor where high humidity may be a factor, ask for the tempered. Like plywood, a popular sheet size is 4' by 8' but smaller panels are available.

PARTICLEBOARD

Particleboard is also a "wood" panel made by combining flakes, chips, and shavings of wood with resins and sizing compounds and then pressing them into panels. The basic wood shape in some of these may be uniform throughout while in others, depending on the process followed, the panel may actually be a ply-board with a central core of coarse flakes sandwiched between layers of fine particles to produce a smoother face-surface.

Today it is used mainly for furniture core stock and floor underlayment. As a core stock it is used for slabs on tables, bureaus, and many other products which are basically case construction. It can be dadoed, routed, shaped, cut, etc., with the same tools used for natural wood. Like hardboard, it is abrasive and will dull tools faster but good strides have been made in making it less abrasive than it used to be.

It is being used as a core stock for wall paneling and for doors, this because its dimensional stability is good and its smooth surfaces are ideal for laminated decorative face materials. Panels have been used in a natural state, like a plywood panel, for dividers, and it is occasionally used as shelves.

WAFERBOARD

An improved form of reconstituted-wood panel is waferboard, which combines fairly large hardwood and softwood chips with resins to make structural-strength sheets in the standard 4x8-foot size. Waferboard can be cut, nailed, sanded, glued and generally worked like plywood, and panels are available in the same ¼ ″ x ¾ ″ range. It has many advantages over plywood in that its uniformly dense composition has no core voids or knotholes, and its edges provide a better holding surface for nails or screws. And, unlike hardboard or particleboard, panels of waferboard contain a higher wood-to-resin ratio, making it lighter and easier to saw and sand. Waferboard also differs from other composition boards in that it is suitable for exterior use.

CONSTRUCTION

BROAD SURFACES—SLABS

In furniture construction, any broad surface is a slab. A frame with an inserted panel can be a slab. Certainly desk tops, table tops, chest tops may be called slabs. Even doors and horizontal and vertical dividers may fall into such a category. Some projects may be composed entirely of slabs.

A slab may be solid lumber—a large piece made by edge-gluing separate pieces of stock. It may be a framed plywood-panel or a plywood-panel inserted into two vertical posts.

A 4′-by-8′ sheet of plywood can be cut up into various-sized slabs to suit a particular project. Plywood can be obtained in various thicknesses from any lumber-yard dealer. This is not true of lumber. You'll find 1 ″ and 2 ″ stock anywhere, but ask for some ½ ″ or ¼ ″ lumber and chances are, if you insist on having it, it will have to be planed down for you at additional cost.

You can always gain, time-wise, by choosing plywood over lumber if for no other reason than the fact that plywood comes ready to cut up. Before you can size lumber slabs you'll have to go through the preliminaries of creating the slab.

Chances are that with most projects you will work with both plywood and lumber and possibly some other slab material such as hardboard or particleboard. When combining materials be sure that the end result is harmonious. In some areas this is not so critical. A case back does not have to match the surface veneer or the solid-lumber material of the case top. Drawer bottoms and dust panels, and certainly cleats and glue blocks, do not have to match the materials used in visible areas.

SOLID LUMBER

Wide pieces of solid lumber are usually built up by gluing together comparatively narrow strips. There are two important reasons for this: Wide boards are rare and would be expensive. The widest boards you are likely to find in a local lumber yard would be 12 ″. The second reason is, wide boards are more likely to warp than narrow ones. You must know from experience that even a 12 ″ board can distort considerably; sometimes to the point where it becomes impractical to use it as is. So, of necessity and for good craftsmanship, you glue up narrow boards to make wide ones.

Here is a simple example of how to

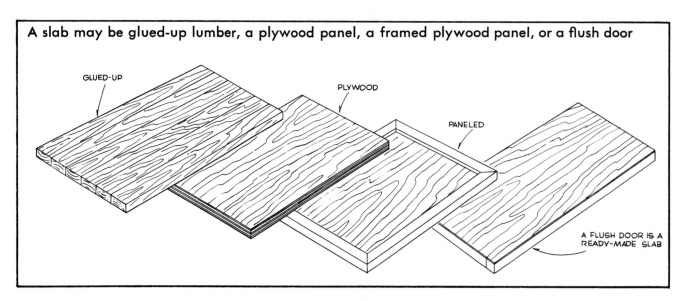

A slab may be glued-up lumber, a plywood panel, a framed plywood panel, or a flush door

GLUED-UP

PLYWOOD

PANELED

A FLUSH DOOR IS A READY-MADE SLAB

Here is how the components of a desk would be laid out on a 4-by-8 plywood panel to assure maximum use of the material and consistent grain direction. To use plywood panels most efficiently and most economically, cut cardboard pieces to represent the various parts of the project and plan the cuts beforehand on paper. Now is the time to plan grain direction and to utilize fully the entire panel.

GRAIN DIRECTION

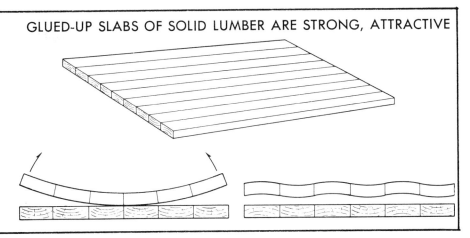

GLUED-UP SLABS OF SOLID LUMBER ARE STRONG, ATTRACTIVE

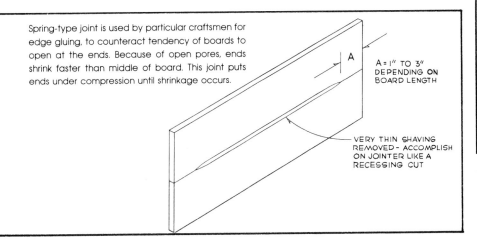

When gluing up boards to make a slab, alternate end grain of each board (right) so warping is confined to individual boards. (Warping is exaggerated in drawing.) After finishing with sander or planer, slab will be flat and smooth. If end grain of each board faces in same direction (left), warping is cumulative and affects the entire slab.

Spring-type joint is used by particular craftsmen for edge gluing, to counteract tendency of boards to open at the ends. Because of open pores, ends shrink faster than middle of board. This joint puts ends under compression until shrinkage occurs.

A = 1″ TO 3″ DEPENDING ON BOARD LENGTH

VERY THIN SHAVING REMOVED – ACCOMPLISH ON JOINTER LIKE A RECESSING CUT

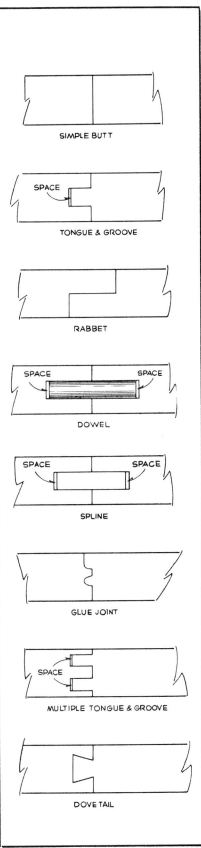

SIMPLE BUTT

SPACE
TONGUE & GROOVE

RABBET

SPACE   SPACE
DOWEL

SPACE   SPACE
SPLINE

GLUE JOINT

SPACE
MULTIPLE TONGUE & GROOVE

DOVE TAIL

The simple butt joint (top) is adequate for most edge-gluing work, but for added strength and tighter fit, you can choose from any of these other joints. The dowel joint is favored by many because of its simplicity and holding power.

balance the stresses in a glued-up slab and thus eliminate or minimize the chances for distortion. Take a 12″ board and rip it into three equal widths. Then take the center piece and invert it, and edge-glue the three pieces back into a solid slab. What this does is alternate the direction of the annual rings from piece to piece; thus the stresses oppose each other to balance out instead of cooperating to cause warpage. This is a typical procedure and should be followed regardless of the width of the individual pieces or of the ultimate width of the slab.

At the same time, give attention to the grain pattern. Place pieces loosely together and study the effect. They can be moved or shifted end-wise. This will also determine which will be the face side of the slab. With the decision made, draw a light pencil line across the pieces and number each one. This will establish position and order.

The ends of the boards, with their open pores, will have more tendency to shrink than the center. To combat this, a slim shaving is taken from the edges that will be glue-coated. This "spring-type" joint puts the ends of the boards under compression so that eventual shrinkage at those points won't result in distortion. It also results in a very thin glue line. It's a procedure for particular craftsmen but it should not be overdone. The shaving removed should be very fine and is best accomplished with a sharp hand-plane. See drawing for more details.

Boards for edge-gluing should be trim and square before gluing. Don't depend on clamps to pull pieces into alignment since this will only create stresses which may eventually cause joint-gaps and other faults.

The joint you use does not have to be fancy. The drawings show many possibilities and each of these is especially suitable for a particular application, but for general work the dowel joint is always a good bet. Be sure to use dowels which are grooved or spiraled and which will fit easily in the holes drilled for them. There must be opportunity for the escape of excess glue and trapped air.

Clamping pressure should be sufficient to bring the edges into firm contact. Use a damp cloth to remove squeezed-out glue immediately; this, to avoid staining the wood but also so you can examine the joints for tightness. Clamping pressure should be uniform over the length of the slab. If possible, use clamps every 10″ or 12″ and alternate them over and under the work. To keep the work flat, use cleats across the surface and clamp these also.

The drawings show methods which can be used to hide the exposed grain at slab-ends. Many of the techniques described for banding, bulking, framing, and joining plywood slabs also apply to solid slab construction.

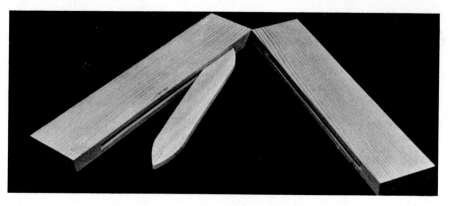

Heavy spline makes a good edge joint for gluing up stock. Note the boat shape of the spline, to conform to the arc left by the saw blade when cutting the groove.

Heavy slab of glued-up stock, which might be used for a workbench top, can be strengthened considerably with a bolt or a threaded rod with a washer and nut at each end. Holes are bored through individual boards before gluing.

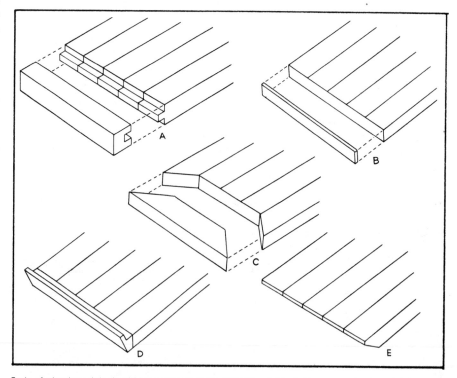

Ends of glued-up slab should be concealed for attractive finish. A. Tongue-and-groove joint in solid stock. B. Simple banding, similar to technique used for plywood. C. Solid insert for a decorative pattern. D. Raised lip, perhaps for a coffee table. E. Beveled edge hides joints beneath line of sight.

RAILS AND FRAMES

RAILS

In actual practice, a rail is a bar of wood (or other material) which joins two other pieces. The assembly which is usually called "leg-and-rail" is a fairly basic piece of design which is applicable, in one form or another, to many kinds of projects. The peripheral pieces on a paneled slab might also be called rails although the four pieces, as a whole, would be a frame. There are times when a rail is not a rail but an "apron" even though its shape, method of joining, and its purpose remain fairly consistent. An apron (sometimes called a skirt) is a horizontal bar of wood which extends between the tops of legs or feet. Examples are the bottom of a chair seat, the underside of a table, the bottom of a chest, etc. The distinction between rail and apron (or skirt) seems to be whether the part is placed high enough (in the case of legs) to touch the slab under which it is placed. It seems to have become an arbitrary decision or maybe just a case of semantics, but be that as it may and call the horizontal bar one or the other, the important consideration as far as construction is concerned is that these are basically "strength" pieces. They are major factors in the durability of a project and therefore must join other pieces in a manner that will provide maximum strength.

RAILS FORM THE DIVIDING ELEMENTS THAT SUPPORT DRAWERS

WITH OR WITHOUT DUST PANELS

Even simple joints can be easily reinforced for strength. Here a notched joint is strengthened with a dowel which is in turn locked with a nail. On thin stock it is a good idea to drill lead holes for the nails.

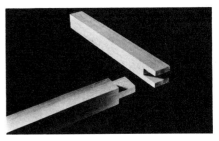

A tenon joint is easy to make with either dado head or saw blade. Make the tenon one-third the thickness of the stock.

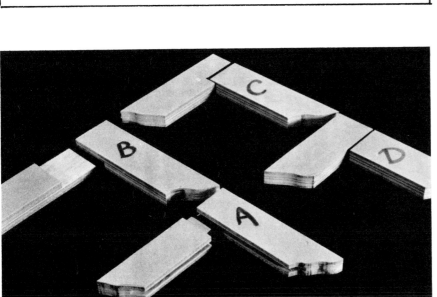

Examples of other end-joints that can be used on rails. A. This joint, which has already been seen, is simply a groove running along the inside edges of the side rails into which the tongues cut in the end rails fit. B. Half-lap joint. C. Notched rail. D. Simple butt joint.

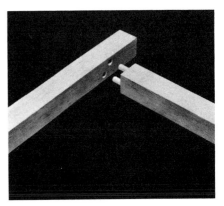

The dowel joint is always reliable. Two dowels are always better than one; they prevent the piece from twisting.

Methods of attaching rail-assemblies to the sides of a case . . .

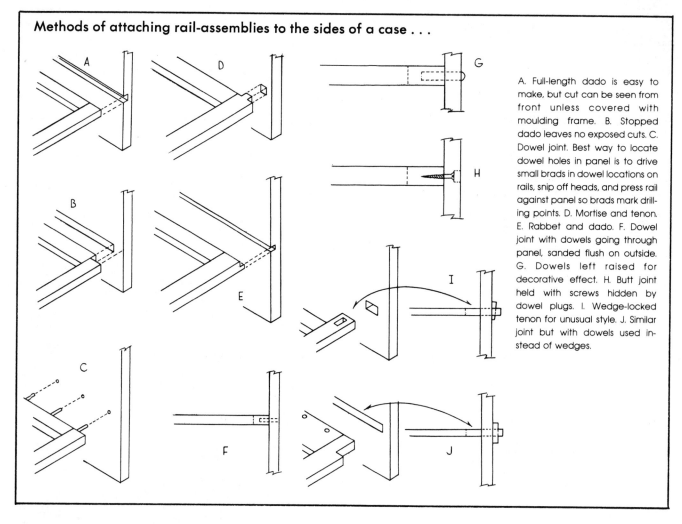

A. Full-length dado is easy to make, but cut can be seen from front unless covered with moulding frame. B. Stopped dado leaves no exposed cuts. C. Dowel joint. Best way to locate dowel holes in panel is to drive small brads in dowel locations on rails, snip off heads, and press rail against panel so brads mark drilling points. D. Mortise and tenon. E. Rabbet and dado. F. Dowel joint with dowels going through panel, sanded flush on outside. G. Dowels left raised for decorative effect. H. Butt joint held with screws hidden by dowel plugs. I. Wedge-locked tenon for unusual style. J. Similar joint but with dowels used instead of wedges.

Plywood panel inserted in a frame can also serve as a slab

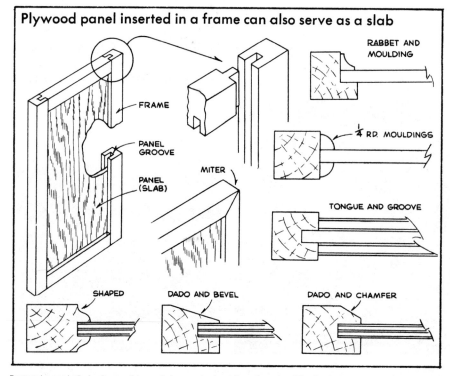

Framed panel eliminates problem of plywood edges. Panel can be fitted to frame in several ways, and frame can be treated decoratively with mouldings or by shaping.

FRAMES

In this category of ''frames'' we include the skeleton frame, which is basically a system of rails on which to hang a cover material; and the solid frame, which is typified by the assembly of top, bottom, and side slabs in a case.

Skeleton Frame. This type of frame can be used on free-standing pieces although its use doesn't seem to make much sense when plywood and similar slab materials are so widely available and in such variety. In this regard the frame provides the strength and so serves to permit the use of thin materials too weak to stand alone or too fine for conventional joinery. When a particularly intriguing, but thin, slab material is available, the choice of a skeleton frame may be one of necessity. It *can* be economical since the frame pieces will be covered, thus permitting the use of cheap, although sound, material; and thin slabs (used as the cover material) are cheaper than thick slabs.

It is not a means of doing a job faster; it certainly isn't a procedure that permits less careful craftsmanship even though it might let you get away with less attention to details and with easier-to-do joints since nails, screws, glue-blocks, and corrugated fasteners could be used and then hidden.

The skeleton frame is more applicable in built-ins where an existing floor, wall, or ceiling is utilized as a component of the project.

Solid Frame. The assembly of slabs which requires no support other than the joints which bond the parts together and which may be further strengthened by the addition of other components such as shelves, dividers, stiles, etc., is a more practical and more acceptable method of forming the frame which is the basic form for all case-goods. In picturing a frame as being those pieces which comprise the top, bottom and sides or ends of a case, we need consider only those two areas where these parts are joined: where the bottom connects to the sides; where the top connects to the sides.

When the frame corners are flush, joint considerations are pretty much the same although the top joints often receive more attention than the bottom ones. Different methods are used when the top slab projects beyond the sides and front. Quite often in this situation, the strength and rigidity of the frame is in the joints which connect sides to bottom and midway components to sides. Thus, if the top is put in place merely with a few screws to keep it in position, the frame as a whole will still have sufficient strength.

THIN SLABS OVER A SKELETON FRAME FORM A CASE

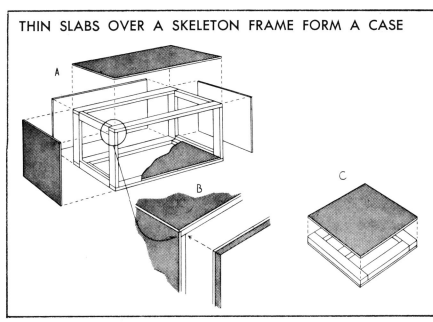

A. Example of skeleton frame for a case. Covering material is glued and mechanically fastened. B. Front edges may be banded with similar material. C. Panels may be attached to skeleton frames and then used as solid slabs.

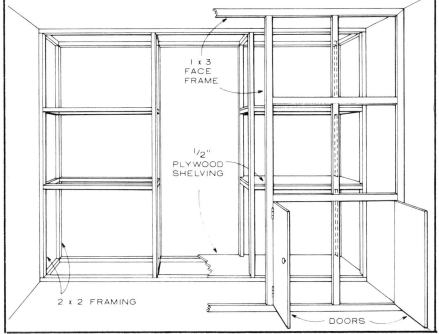

Skeleton frame can be used to construct a built-in that covers the entire wall of a room. Some of the frame members are used here as supports for the shelves. Face frame of 1-by-3s serves as a surface for hanging doors that enclose the unit.

Skeleton frame joint construction.

Joints used in constructing a skeleton frame must be just as strong as those used elsewhere, even though appearance is not as important. This joins parts going in three directions.

Cover material can be applied with nails or with glue or contact cement when appearance is paramount. Front edges would be banded with same material to conceal joints and grain.

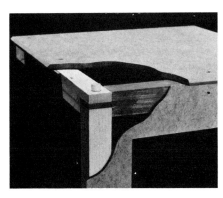

Here is the same joint, as above but the addition of a lock-dowel makes it impossible for the pieces to separate. Drill the hole for the dowel while parts are held in correct position–by clamping or nailing if necessary.

DRAWERS

The basic form of a drawer is a box without a top. If all you had to consider was strength, then it's conceivable that thick lumber, mated with butt joints and reinforced with glue, nails, screws, and glue-blocks, would be successful. If you were going to store cotton balls and appearance was not a factor, you could get along with an apple crate, or you could store handkerchiefs in a cigar box. There really are times when these examples could be used quite nicely, if the location and the project and the storage items permit it; but in furniture, refinements made necessary by practical and esthetic considerations are definitely in order.

Stress in a drawer is mostly down on the drawer bottom because of the drawer contents and at the points where the drawer front is joined to the sides. When you open a drawer you are, in effect, attempting to pull off the drawer front. To avoid this, the front-to-sides joints should be strong and should, preferably, lock. That's why quality furniture buyers look for the dovetail at these points. A discriminating buyer might even be disappointed if the drawer *back* was not dovetailed.

The dovetail is an excellent example of a joint which will hold together even when the glue fails. But it is not the only joint with such characteristics. Actually, it should not be the paramount factor in judging over-all furniture quality since modern machinery will turn out dovetails like a machine extruding spaghetti. You will find dovetails even on cheap furniture.

The drawer sides can be thinner—⅝″ or

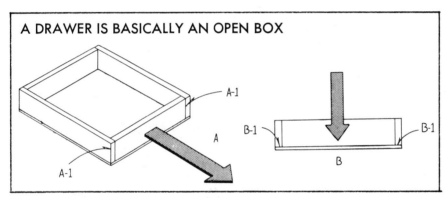

A DRAWER IS BASICALLY AN OPEN BOX

Aside from appearance, there are two important reasons why drawer is not as simple to construct as the box above. Pulling out a drawer (A), creates strain at points A-1; and loading a drawer (B) creates strain at points B-1. Use strong joints at these places.

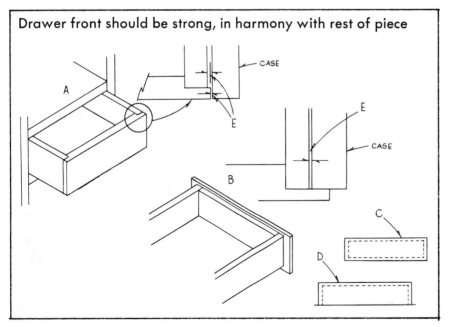

Drawer front should be strong, in harmony with rest of piece

Front can be flush with the case edges (A) or overlap edges (B). By using a second piece, front can overlap on four edges (C) or on three (D). Provide clearance of $\frac{1}{16}$″ (E) so drawer will work smoothly.

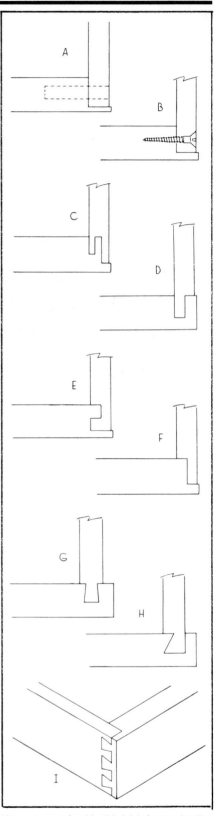

Here are some front-to-side joints for constructing drawers: A. Pegged joint with dowels. B. Simple rabbet reinforced with nails or screws. C. Combination groove and rabbet joint. D. Rabbet and dado joint. E. Another type of rabbet and dado joint. F. Side rabbeted joint. G. Dovetail and dovetail slot. H. Half-dovetail. I. Dovetail–exposed or blind.

Methods of attaching drawer back

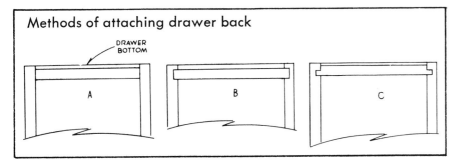

A. Simple butt joint. B. Dado. C. Dado and rabbet.

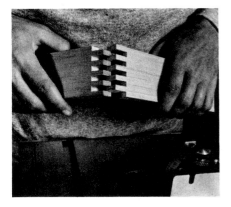

Finger-lap joint (left) is sometimes used on drawer backs, provides lots of gluing area. Joint can be locked with a dowel tapped into a hole drilled not greater than half the thickness of the stock (right).

Methods of attaching drawer bottom

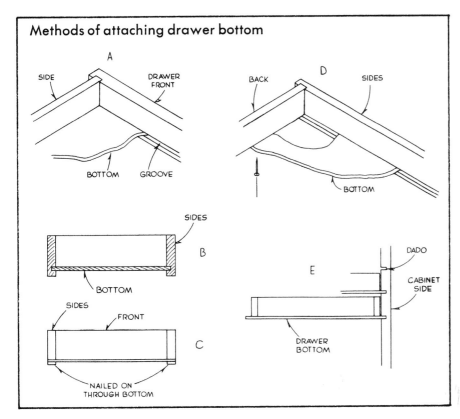

Bottom can be of hardboard, between ⅛" and ½" thick, and let into grooves in the front and sides (A and B). Drawer back is cut narrower than the sides, and bottom is nailed to its edge (D). If only hand tools are available, strips can be nailed through bottom into sides (C). Extended bottoms (E) provide slides to fit in dadoes in cabinet sides—a good idea for small shop drawers.

½" stock—but here too the material used should be strong. Relieve or at least round off the top edges of the side pieces. The drawer bottom should be let in to the drawer sides and also the front. Thickness of the bottom piece depends on the size of the drawer and what you will store in it, but ⅛" is about a minimum. A ¼" thickness is better; if necessary, you can go as high as ½". Hardboard is a good material for drawer bottoms because it is stiff, smooth and doesn't warp.

The thickness of the drawer back can match the drawer sides. It should, preferably, be let in to dado cuts formed in the side pieces.

All inside and outside surfaces of drawer parts should be carefully sanded and, at least, sealed. Surfaces should feel smooth to the touch; all edges should be slightly rounded by working them with sandpaper.

INSTALLING DRAWERS

Installation of a drawer means the method used to guide it smoothly in and out of the opening. There are many ways to do this, and the methods range from the use of ready-made hardware with wheels and rollers to no guides at all—simply a box sliding in a box. The *classic* method, and one which you will find on most quality furniture, employs a guide which is attached to the case or frame, and a runner or slide which is attached to the drawer.

The guide is a straight, smooth bar of wood firmly attached at each end and carefully positioned so the drawer will not rub against the sides of the case. The slide is a similar piece of wood, broader than, and grooved to fit over, the guide. These pieces do not require bulk; their purpose is to guide, not carry, the weight of the drawer. In the most common application, the guide is rabbeted at each end and attached to the front and rear rails of the frame with a touch of glue and a few nails, or maybe a single screw at each end. The slide is glued to the drawer bottom with possibly a nail angle-driven into the drawer front and another into the drawer back. You can dispense with the glue if you attach the slide firmly to the front and rear drawer components. When the drawer back extends below the drawer bottom, the back must be notched so the slide can be fitted.

When the case has no horizontal frames, this system of course can't be used since there is no place to attach the guide. Then guides and runners must be attached to the sides of the drawer and to the inner surfaces of the case. Common method is to attach cleats (guides) to the case sides and to groove the drawer sides. Thus you have a guide-and-slide arrangement, but in this situation the entire weight of the drawer and its contents is on the cleat, with the drawer side also coming in for its share of the stress. This could be reversed by putting the cleat on the drawer side and forming the grooves in the case side. One basis for making the choice is whether the drawer fronts will be flush with the case edges or whether they will lip over. When they are flush, it's better to attach the guide cleats to the case and groove the drawer sides. When the drawer front has a lip which will conceal the case edges you can use the alternate method.

When the design puts the stress on the guide-and-slide, then the ultimate use of the drawer is an important factor in determining the size of the cleat used as the guide. For example, a ¼″ square piece of pine may do nicely as the guide for a drawer in which you will store handkerchiefs, but certainly not for a shop drawer that will hold heavy tools. The sketches in this section will show other methods as well as some variations of the more commonly used techniques.

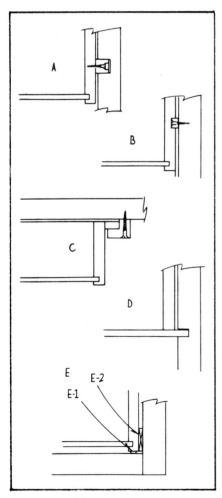

Methods of installing drawers: A. Runner screwed to drawer side rides in dado cut in case side. B. Reverse of A; dado cut in drawer rides on runner screwed to case. C. Drawer hung on rabbeted strip, runner attached to drawer sides. D. Extended drawer bottom rides in dadoes cut in case sides. E. Drawer rides on dome glides (E-1), guided by strip (E-2) attached to drawer side.

HOW TO INSTALL DRAWERS IN A CHEST

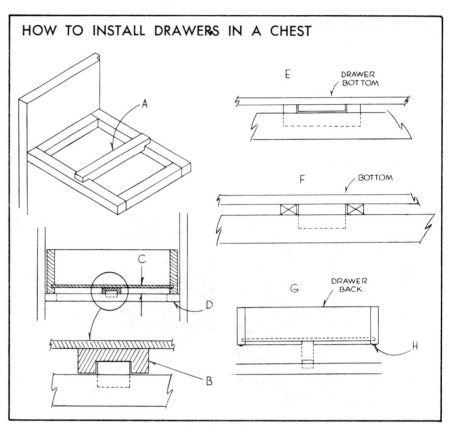

Guide bar (A) is rabbet cut at ends to fit over front and back rails. U-shaped runner (B) is attached to drawer bottom with nails or screws at front and back. Thickness of guide and runner must be such that drawer rests on its sides (D). To minimize dimension C, you can use a channel as the guide and a plain strip of wood as the runner (E), or use two strips as a guide (F). You can also notch the drawer back (G) and let it act as the runner. Thumb tacks (H) help drawer to slide smoothly.

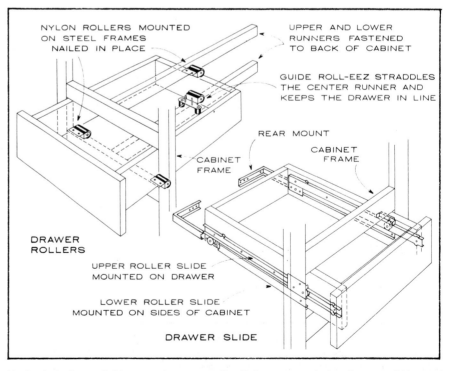

Mechanical rollers and slides ease drawer operation. Rollers are mounted on the case dividers and drawer runners. Various types of slides are available. This one mounts on drawer and on case sides. Some have rear mounts (shown) which can be attached to the case back where sides are lacking.

DOORS

A door doesn't add structural strength to a project but it can add, or detract, from its appearance and it can make the project more, or less, convenient to use. The door, if it is a fabricated component, must be a strong assembly in itself, and the method used to install it must be firm and durable.

Most doors are slabs—framed or unframed—but they can be many other things. Slim slats can be assembled in a vertical pattern to make tambour doors that will turn corners. Sections can be hinged so they will fold back on themselves. Horizontal slats can be inserted in frames to make louvered doors, or you can combine louvers with slabs. Decorator effects or particular style treatments are achieved by the shape of frame pieces when inserted slabs are used or when mouldings are used to create a pattern on a slab. Pierced effects are possible on solid slabs or by assembling pre-cut, narrow pieces; you can even "weave" a door by using thin and narrow strips of wood.

Doors can swing on hinges, slide in grooves, fold back on themselves, even disappear. And sometimes, as in the case of drop doors, they may also serve as a writing or serving surface. Doors on most furniture pieces either swing or slide.

HINGED DOORS

Hinged doors give maximum accessibility to contents but they require room in which to swing them open. Sliding doors do not require "swing" room but they reduce accessibility by 50 percent. When the normal swing for hinged doors is a problem and sliding doors just won't do, you can consider using hinges at the top or the bottom of the door. In such a case the door could be opened wide even if the project was hemmed in on both sides by adjacent walls or other furniture.

Hinges may be used on framed or unframed door slabs and the door itself may be set in flush with the case edges, or butted against the case edges; or it could be a combination of both such as the "cabinet-door lip," which is basically a rabbet cut.

Most any slab material can be used to make a door. Thin, ready-made slab materials are ideal for sliding doors and for framed, panel doors. These materials include plywood, hardboards (plain, perforated, or pierced), particleboard, laminates, etc. You can make a thick door and do it economically by covering both sides of a frame with one of the above-mentioned materials—a hollow-core construction. At times, it's possible to get away with covering just one side. A perforated hardboard can be very functional when used on the back of a door since, when

used with clips and hooks made for the purpose, it provides ready-to-use storage facilities. Most of the ideas and techniques described for forming framed slabs can be used to make doors.

Solid-lumber doors are formed in the manner described for making solid-lumber slabs. Be especially careful about making them from many narrow pieces rather than a few wide ones since doors must be self-sufficient and all construction must serve to prevent warpage. Solid-lumber doors may also be formed by assembling boards vertically with horizontal cleats (or battens) across the back to secure them. The door boards do not have to be edge-glued but the mating edges should be matched to minimize (visually) any separation that might occur. The matching can be done with a tongue-and-groove or with rabbet cuts or with any of the joints described in a previous section. On utility jobs where you don't wish to bother with either edge-gluing or matching, you can achieve a similar result by chamfering the top corners of the mating edges.

We might mention a kind of slab-on-slab idea which makes it possible to achieve a rabbeted edge (cabinet-door lip) without having to shape it with saw blade, shaper, or router. Basically, the idea is this: Cut one

slab to fit *inside* the door opening. Then cut a second slab of thinner material that overlaps the case edges. Bonding the second slab to the first one gives you a door, in effect, with a rabbeted edge. Instead of a base slab, you could use an open frame. An open frame could also be covered on both sides—the back cover to match the frame dimensions, the front to extend and so form the rabbet.

HINGES AND THEIR INSTALLATION

The hinge must bear the weight of the door plus whatever else is on the door, and it must do this through countless openings and closings. If a lead hole for screws is needed, keep it as small as possible so the screws will grip with maximum strength. Two hinges will usually do the job, but if the door is unusually heavy or large, then install a third hinge at the center. A 1" butt hinge will do for most furniture projects since doors are seldom more than 2' wide. Consider a 2" butt hinge for doors over this. Closet doors, room doors, and doors on large built-ins may require a 3" hinge.

Butt Hinges. Hinges may be concealed, semiconcealed, or surface-mounted. Often, hinges together with other matching hardware are used as decorative details. The butt hinge is usually installed so the pin loops are visible from the front. This means, when a door is inset, that one leaf of the hinge is at-

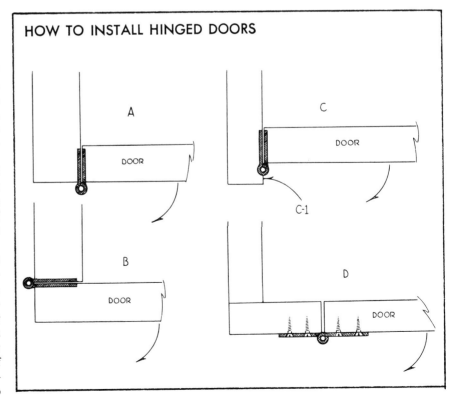

HOW TO INSTALL HINGED DOORS

A

DOOR

B

DOOR

C

DOOR

C-1

D

DOOR

Four basic ways to hang doors with butt hinges: A. Door flush with case edge, hinges mortised. B. Door overlapping case edge, hinges mortised. C. Door inset beyond case edge, hinges mortised, C-1 is natural stop. D. Door flush with case edge, hinges surface-mounted.

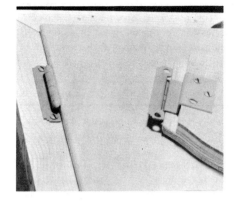

Semiconcealed offset hinges are used on lipped doors, shown here back and front to demonstrate proper method of installation. Door may be lipped by cutting a rabbet around its edge, or by attaching a thin panel of slightly larger dimensions.

tached to the case side (or the frontal frame), the other to the door edge. In order to reduce the gap between door edge and case side, both components are mortised. The length of the mortise (or the ''gain'' as it is sometimes called) should be as long as the hinge. The width of the mortise should equal the width of one hinge-leaf but only to the base of the pin loops. The depth of the mortise should equal the thickness of the hinge-leaf—no more, no less.

Best bet for accurate installation is to put the door in the opening (holding it with slim wedges if necessary) and to mark both door and case for hinge location. Then remove the door and use the hinge itself as a template to mark the mortise areas. *Be especially careful about depth.* The mortise may be cleaned out quickly if you have a portable router. Otherwise use a sharp knife to outline the cut and a chisel to remove the waste. If you do get into trouble with the mortise depth, you can compensate (if too deep) by using paper or thin cardboard under the hinge. Take your time when installing hinges, no matter what kind. Messy workmanship here can interfere with smooth operation of the door, may make repair work necessary, and may detract from the appearance of the entire project.

Offset Hinges. These are used to hang lipped doors. The important consideration is that the rabbet cut in the door should match the amount of offset in the hinge. A common error is to arbitrarily cut the rabbet and then try to find a hinge to suit. While offset hinges are made in different sizes, they are not available to match *every* situation. Have the hinges on hand before you cut. Offset hinges are available in many styles for either surface-mounting or semiconcealment.

Other types of hinges are shown in the drawings and some of the photos will show the installation of the Soss hinge, which is truly an invisible hinge and quite simple to use.

Single doors must be stopped at case edge

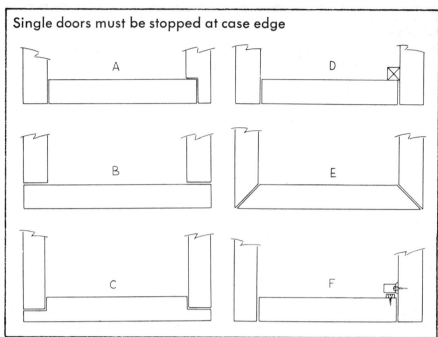

A. Door flush with case can be stopped by rabbeting case edge. B. Overlapping door stopped by case edge. C. Door rabbeted on four sides. D. Wooden or metal cleat used as a stop. E. Mitered door edge stopped by matching cut in case edge. F. Magnetic catch both stops door and holds it closed.

Double doors present another problem

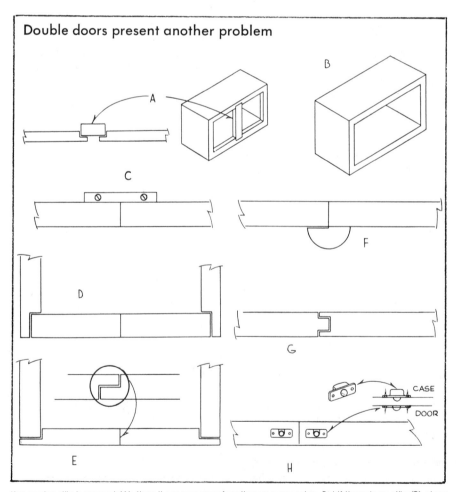

If a center-stile is present (A), then it serves some function as case edge. But if there is no stile (B), door can be stopped by: C. Cleat screwed to top or bottom of case. D. Rabbeted case edge. E. Rabbeted door edge. F. Wooden moulding. G. Tongue and groove in door edges. H. Bullet catch.

SLIDING DOORS

Sliding doors are very popular on contemporary pieces and easy to make and install whether you work with hand or power tools. Major objection is that they cut down on accessibility of the project's contents by 50 percent, but this is important only if 100 percent accessibility is necessary at any given time. If it is not important, this objection may be disregarded.

There are many factors in favor of sliding doors. As we said, they are easy to make and install. Also, they permit the use of materials too thin to be practical for hinged doors. The making of a sliding door involves no more than cutting a ready-made slab material to length and width. Installation requires forming grooves or attaching tracks. Hardware may be as simple as a set of flush pulls.

Plywood, hardboard, particleboard, laminates—all make good sliding doors, and since these are available in softwoods, hardwoods, and plastics and, in some materials, with a variety of surface textures, you have an easy means of enhancing the appearance of a project. Some materials, such as glass, which would be extremely difficult for the homecraftsman to hang on hinges, become available as door material when you think of them as sliding units. Glass, for example, especially if the edges are ground, can do quite well in wooden tracks or grooves cut in the case. For more durability, or smoother action if necessary, you can use metal tracks that you can buy. These may be surface-mounted or recessed in grooves so they are less visible.

Sliding doors seldom require lock-or-catch hardware and then it's usually installed for security reasons. And we have already mentioned the fact that, unlike hinged doors, sliding doors do not require "swing" and so cut down on the amount of room needed *around* a project after it's moved from the shop to the house.

Grooves for sliding doors can be formed right in the case members, or in a frontal frame if one is used. The grooves do not have to be deep; often ⅛" is sufficient. Width of the grooves should be a little more than the thickness of the door stock so the doors will move easily. To make sliding doors removable, the top groove must be deeper than the bottom one. This makes sense for two reasons: it is conceivable that you may wish to remove the doors; and it will not be necessary to install the doors when you are assembling the case members—you merely add them at the tail-end of the job.

SLIDING DOORS ARE EASY TO MAKE AND INSTALL

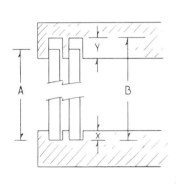

To make sliding doors removable, use this formula: Y equals 2X; A equals B minus X. Grooves for sliding doors may be cut directly into the top and bottom edges of the cabinet case (center photo). The wall separating the grooves should not be thinner than ⅛", but it should not be too thick or it wastes space. Grooves may also be cut into the front face-frame of the case, if one is used. Groove depth should be kept to a minimum to avoid weakening the frame.

You can also form the grooves for sliding doors by attaching cleats, as at left, or by using specially made tracks of wood or metal available at most building-supply stores. If you want sliding doors to be flush with the edge of the case, form a tongue on the outer door edge which rides in a matching groove in the case. This may require using thicker material for the doors, as there must be ample surface to cut the tongue.

Grooves are needed at the top and the bottom; they are not necessary at the sides and so are often omitted there. But running the grooves completely around will pay off in two ways; all door edges, except the center ones, will be encased in grooves when the doors are closed, creating a dust seal; and the side groove will help conceal any distracting gaps when a door is carelessly closed.

Special sliding-door hardware, consisting of metal tracks and wheels, is available but is necessary mostly on closets and large built-ins. With accessory materials of this type, complete instructions for correct installation are included in the package.

FOLDING DOORS

Folding doors seem more practical for large openings in closets, built-ins, passageways between rooms, and for use as dividers between living areas. When considering such applications it is best to buy the special installation hardware which is available and to follow the instructions supplied with it. You can make your own hollow-core slabs or buy narrow, ready-made doors to hinge for folding. You can even buy a ready-to-install unit, a covered, special mechanism which folds like an accordion so that even a large door occupies very little space when closed. On furniture, the folding door does not require the swing space needed by hinged doors and, when open, will reveal more of the project's contents than possible with sliding doors.

Basically, folding doors are made by hinging vertical pieces so they may fold back on each other. The outside piece is hinged to the case side; the inside piece is pinned to ride a groove cut in the case. On small projects you can get away with a single groove cut in the case bottom; on larger projects it's best to use a groove at the top also. It's also possible to use a track at the top with a T-shaped pin in the door. Thus, the door would actually hang from, and be supported by, the track.

On small projects the pin-and-groove technique works fine and, actually, it is recommended that such designs be confined to small openings so that the hinge on the case will be ample to support the weight of the sections. The pin, then, acts merely as a guide. On long openings it's a good idea to install a pin at the top of every second vertical piece; this will help to insure a folding action.

DROP DOORS

Drop doors can be handy when you don't have swing room for hinged doors and when sliding (or folding doors) won't do, but a more usual application for a drop door is typified by a wall-hung desk where the door drops down to become the writing surface.

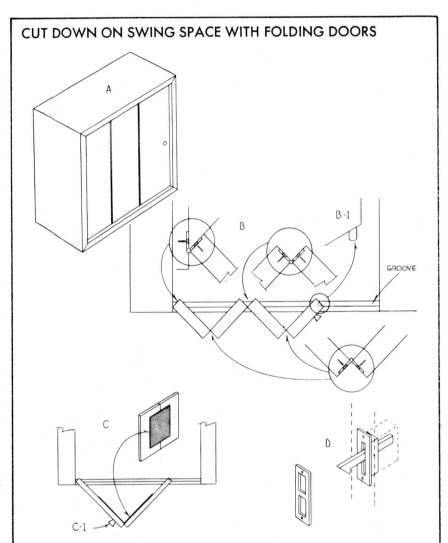

CUT DOWN ON SWING SPACE WITH FOLDING DOORS

A. Folding doors are vertical panels that move like accordion pleats. B. You can make folding doors with any slab material and butt hinges. Note hinge placement and mortising. Guide pin (B-1) rides in a groove at top and bottom of case. C. For narrower openings, a two-panel door is sufficient. Here you can use glued-on canvas or self-adhesive felt instead of hinges. D. Folding doors can be held closed with this type of catch.

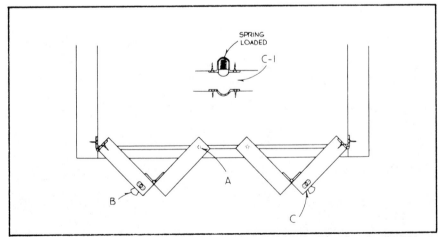

Bi-fold doors open away from each other. Hinges connecting the doors to the case must be mortised, but the panel-joint hinges may be surface-mounted. Guide-pin (A) is also used, but unless doors are very large and heavy only one—at the bottom—is necessary. Pull (B) should be located at this position on each door. Bullet catch (C) is recommended here. C-1 shows catch in cross-section.

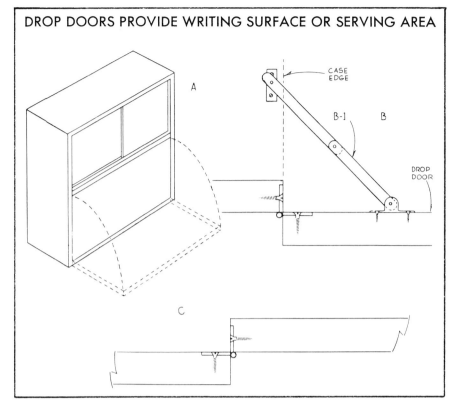

DROP DOORS PROVIDE WRITING SURFACE OR SERVING AREA

Drop door is most often used on a secretary or small wall-hung desk (A). Door may be on outside edge of case (B), with hinges placed as shown. Folding metal support (B-1) is usually used. When door is flush with or recessed inside frame, hinges must be placed as shown at C.

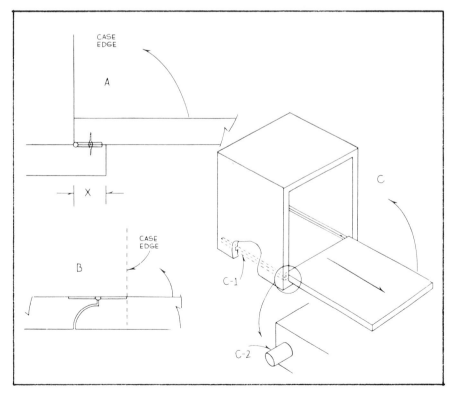

Drop door can be supported without using hardware by (A) providing an overhang (X) on which the door can rest, or (B) shaping the edges in an inverted drop-leaf design. You can also build a combination drop-slide door (C) by cutting a groove (C-1) at the lower sides of the case in which a pivot dowel on the door (C-2) rides. When door is fully extended, it can be tilted into closed position and held by a bullet catch.

On other projects a drop door can provide a serving area.

There are three basic methods of installation: hinges, plus hardware to hold the door horizontal; combination hardware which supplies the hinge action and also acts as a stop; and hinges plus a particular case design so the door will stay horizontal without additional hardware.

It is important to judge just how much weight the door must hold. Hardware can be light or heavy, so you can choose it to support just the weight of the door, or the weight of a person who will lean on it while writing.

TAMBOUR DOORS

Tambour doors have a sliding action but are made by assembling vertical slats on a flexible backing so they can actually slide in a curved groove or even in a full circle. They have a clean, uncluttered look and, like other sliding doors, do not require swing space. They require a groove at both the top and the bottom of the opening and, like a conventional sliding door, can be removable if you make the top groove deeper than the bottom one.

Grooves (at top and bottom) must match perfectly if the doors are to work smoothly. The best idea is to form a pattern (actually a guide-template) which may be used with a router on both top and bottom components. If you are not equipped to form the grooves, you can get by with tracks cut on a bandsaw, jigsaw or by hand.

As the door is moved, each slat runs tangential to the curve, so you can see there is a very definite relationship between thickness of the slat, width of the groove, radius of the curve, and width of the slat. The narrower and thinner the slat, the smaller the curve-radius can be. As it is seldom practical to consider a radius of less than 1½″, this is a good starting point. To plan for your own needs, make a full-size plan view and plot the curve; then you can easily determine the maximum dimensions of the slats. If you have a particular slat material on hand, then simply reverse the procedure. However, it's best to form slats that will fit a practical curve.

Slats can be as simple as flat pieces of wood which you cut from solid stock, or they can be ready-made mouldings or batten strips. Screen-door mouldings and half-round mouldings are two suggestions worthy of investigating for the purpose.

The conventional method of assembling tambour doors calls for canvas and glue. Best bet is to apply the glue to the canvas, wait for it to become tacky, and then place the slats. Of course, it is important that you avoid getting glue between the slats since they must not be attached to each other except by means of the backing canvas. One method we have used with good success is to substitute a self-adhesive felt for the canvas. This material is available in what used to be five-and-ten-cent stores and in craft-and-hobby shops. Since it is pressure-sensitive it eliminates the gooey glue procedure, and—equally important—the door is ready for installation immediately.

Tambour door is shown here riding in bottom groove of case. Backing material is a substitute for a multitude of hinges, keeps slats butted together in a flexible assembly. It is vitally important that top and bottom grooves match.

Be sure to square the slats before you apply the backing. A good way to do this is to place them face-down in the corner formed by the two legs of a carpenter's square. The edge of the first slat rests against one leg of the square, one end of each of the other slats butts against the other leg of the square. If any gaps occur between the slats, you'll know before gluing that the long edges on some of the slats are not parallel. Thus, a correction can be made immediately.

LOUVERED DOORS

Louvered doors may serve merely for appearance or to permit ventilation. In either case, the louvers are placed horizontally in a frame. If the louvers are fixed, they may be set in dadoes cut in the frame pieces. If they are moveable they may be pinned at each end so they can pivot about a central axis. It's not likely that you might ever want to adjust individual louvers; usually, the strips are tied together with a cloth tape or a slim, wooden bar so they may move together. Follow the drawings for essential details.

DOOR HARDWARE

It is quite possible to discover a set of hardware which is so attractive and so intriguing

TAMBOUR DOORS DISAPPEAR AS THEY ARE OPENED

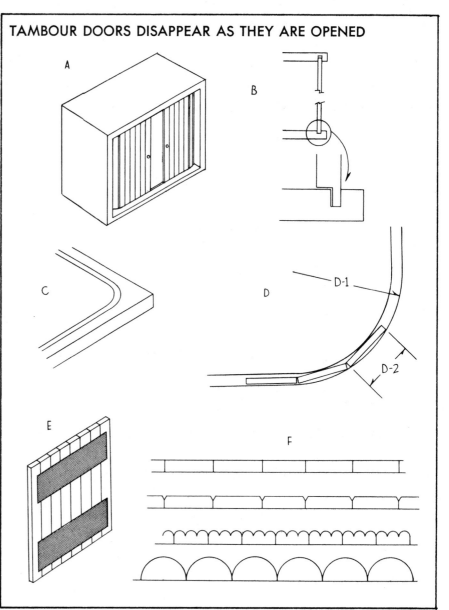

Tambour doors are made of thin slats that slide in curved grooves in the top and bottom of the case (A). Depth of grooves and shape of door edge (B) follow principle of sliding doors. The big difference is the curve in the groove (C). The radius of the turn (D-1) and the width of the slats (D-2), as well as their thickness, must be in proper proportion so that the door has enough freedom to slide smoothly. The slats are assembled with canvas glued across the back (E), or you can use self-adhesive felt. Slats can be square or have chamfered or rounded edges, or you can use ready-made moldings (F).

that it inspires you to build a project on which to hang it. Some Oriental styles rely heavily on large, brass fixtures to help create the over-all effect.

Hardware *is* necessary on many projects, so you must choose it for function. It can perform unobtrusively or it can supply decorative details. Many times shaping a particular area of a component substitutes for hardware. This is especially true on drawer and door pulls.

Aside from the guidance provided by the laws of harmony and good taste, it is difficult to set down hard and fast rules concerning

the choice and the use of hardware. When making a reproduction or working along the lines dictated by a particular furniture style, the choice is made for you. You simply use the hardware called for. For example, you can buy pulls and knobs that are exactly right for Chippendale, French styles, English Regency, Provincial and Contemporary. Many of these may be adapted to styling which is not truly authentic.

You can be more flexible when choosing fixtures for original designs; often the choice is one of personal preference and taste and of the project-image which you see in your own

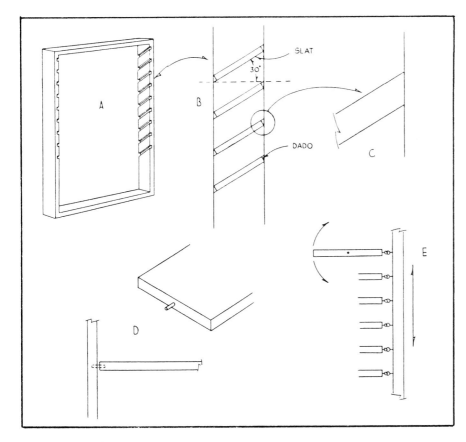

Stationary louver doors are made by cutting angled dadoes in the side members of the door frame (A). Dadoes should be angled at about 30 degrees and the louvers spaced so that the top edge of one louver is on the same line as the bottom edge of the one above (B). Edges of louvers may be beveled so they are flush with the case edge (C) for a neater appearance. Movable louvers (D) are pivoted on a dowel or cut-off nail, opened and closed by a bar tied to each louver front with a screw eye (E).

mind. Cleated board doors with a cabinet-door lip can be mounted with semiconcealed, offset hinges, but since such an assembly is easily associated with rough-hewn and rustic styling, wrought-iron strap hinges would also be compatible.

The project material, to a considerable degree, will automatically influence your choice. Of course this is perfectly logical since you already knew the styling you had in mind or the effect you wished to create before you decided on what material to use. If you were making a dining-room set along provincial lines and decided on knotty pine, you would end up choosing Provincial hardware. Sleek, hardwood plywood automatically affects styling and thus influences hardware selection.

Probably the one rule you can apply generally is to decide whether the hardware is going to be prominent or subdued. You can use a pull on a drawer or a door and it will not attract too much attention, but you can also back up that pull with a fancy escutcheon plate and thus call more attention to it. A cabinet-door lock can function with just a simple hole for the key to enter, or you can use a keyhole escutcheon. Of course, what may appear to be a purely decorative addition may actually serve a very practical function. Escutcheon plates are good examples of this—on a pull or knob they protect the surrounding area and keep it clean; on a keyhole they do the same job.

LEGS

Furniture legs can be simple or complex. They can be straight, turned, or shaped. They can be ready-mades which are simply screw-attached to the underside of a flush door or they can be the extension of a post beyond the bottom of an inserted panel, a construction that is often found on the side components of a chest. But they do have one thing in common—they support the weight of the project plus the weight of people and/or items which are stored in or on the project.

Legs are strongest (and easiest to attach) when they are vertical. The more slant they have, the more stress that is put on the attachment joint and the stronger it should be. Of course, strong joints plus stretchers will permit considerable slant, but the fact that good engineering can make it practical merely means that basic rules can be ignored occasionally if necessary. Generally, it is a good idea to limit slant to a maximum of 15 degrees, and to use this on low items such as coffee tables.

Some legs will take more of a beating than others—even on the same project. In most chairs, for example, the load is greatest over the back legs, especially when the sitter tilts the chair back. In areas such as this, the slant consideration becomes even more important. Often you can create a visual impression of slant by making taper cuts on the inside edges of straight legs, thereby combining the strength of a vertical leg with the appearance of a slanted one.

LEG DESIGN

To simplify the business of leg design and even leg styling, think of the ultimate shape as being a variation or modification of a basic form. A cross-section of the form could be circular, oval, square, rectangular, triangular. A longitudinal cut through the center of a leg could reveal one, several, or all of these shapes; the latter being especially true of turned legs. Even the shape of the cabriole leg will be easier to visualize if you picture it encased in a basic block.

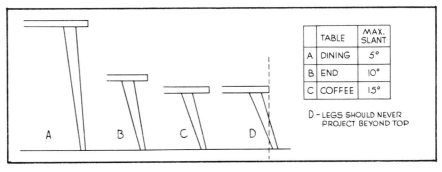

	TABLE	MAX. SLANT
A	DINING	5°
B	END	10°
C	COFFEE	15°

D - LEGS SHOULD NEVER PROJECT BEYOND TOP

Recommended angles for attaching legs to dining table, end table and coffee table.

Almost any power tool can play a part in leg-shaping. Tapers can be formed on a jointer or the tool can be used for stock reduction in a prescribed area. Such a reduction on two adjacent sides and for most of the length of a square would produce a shape with Oriental styling. The table saw will cut square legs and with a special jig can produce tapers. With a moulding head it can do some fluting and reeding; with a dado head (or a moulding head and blank knives) it can be used to reduce stock.

The bandsaw is necessary to produce cabriole shapes and, when size permits, the jigsaw can serve in the same capacity. The lathe is necessary for turned forms and sometimes serves an accessory role for additional details on a form shaped on another machine—a turned club foot on a cabriole leg is one example.

Sometimes a machine is used merely to create a raw form, after which additional shaping, carving, detailing, finishing, etc., are done by hand.

Legs may be attached to rails which are attached to top . . .

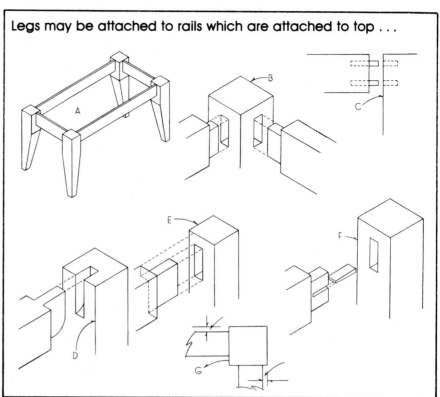

A. Typical leg-and-roll assembly. B. Mortise-tenon joint for attaching legs to rail is strong but should be made on a drill press for best results. C. Dowel joint is easier to make, accomplishes the same thing. D. Stub tenon is easily done with dado on table saw. Note how tenon is shaped to conform with arc left by dado. E. One-sided tenon is useful when rail is of thin material. F. Slotted tenon is locked by wedge for extra strength.

You can cut cabriole legs without a lathe . . .

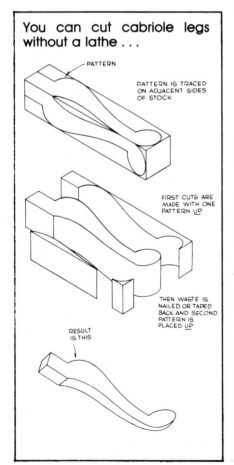

PATTERN

PATTERN IS TRACED ON ADJACENT SIDES OF STOCK

FIRST CUTS ARE MADE WITH ONE PATTERN UP

THEN WASTE IS NAILED OR TAPED BACK AND SECOND PATTERN IS PLACED UP

RESULT IS THIS

Compound cuts on a bandsaw or jigsaw can produce this shapely cabriole leg. First trace the pattern on adjacent sides of the stock, make first cuts with one side up, then replace waste material with glue or tape. Turn stock so other pattern is up and make second cuts.

. . . or attached directly to the underside of the furniture.

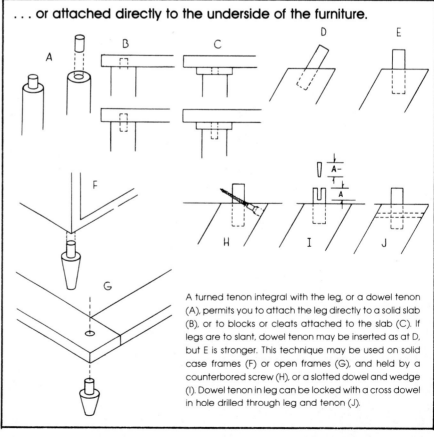

A turned tenon integral with the leg, or a dowel tenon (A), permits you to attach the leg directly to a solid slab (B), or to blocks or cleats attached to the slab (C). If legs are to slant, dowel tenon may be inserted as at D, but E is stronger. This technique may be used on solid case frames (F) or open frames (G), and held by a counterbored screw (H), or a slotted dowel and wedge (I). Dowel tenon in leg can be locked with a cross dowel in hole drilled through leg and tenon (J).

SHELVES

The things you plan to store or display are important factors affecting shelf design. It doesn't much matter whether you are hanging the shelves on a wall, putting them in a free-standing bookcase, or installing them in a cabinet or chest; you must consider the items they will hold in order to use the shelves conveniently and to get maximum space utilization. A series of equally spaced, horizontal slabs is seldom the most efficient answer. Consider books. Eight inches is a good shelf depth (width of slab used) for the average novel but for some books, 12″ is better. Book height is not the only factor to consider when establishing space between shelves; you must also allow for finger room so it's easy to get books out. Spacing of 12″ seems adequate for general use but some books will require more and many will require less. So book shelves should either be adjustable or designed to provide for the variations you will encounter. These considerations point up the value of designing for what you are going to store or display before you start building.

Another bad design feature of fixed and equally spaced shelves is that you limit storage height to that one distance between shelves. By thinking about step shelves, balcony shelves, and triangular shelves (as the drawings show) you provide for storage of items at various heights and the items will be more convenient to get to.

Don't guess at spacing and shelf-depths. When you make a storage project, you know pretty well what you will be using it for. Then you can design by actually measuring the items and by pre-arranging them for space utilization and convenience.

"Floating" shelves are supported by iron rods which are inserted through the wall covering and into the wall studs. Back edge of shelf is drilled to fit over rods. Accurate drilling and good, flat stock are critical factors in getting neat results.

You can make your own shelf supports of wood . . .

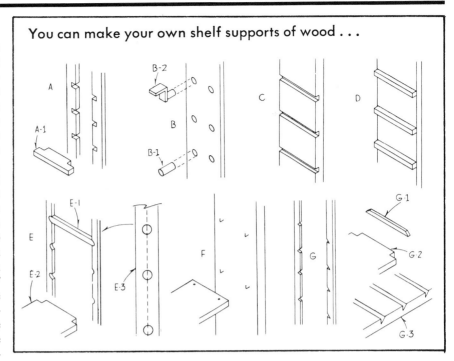

A. Notched strips receive shaped shelf brackets (A-1), or ends of shelves may be so cut and fit into the notches. B. Short dowels (B-1) or ready-made clips (B-2) fit in blind holes and support shelves. C. Shelves fit in dadoes cut in side supports. D. Shelves rest on cleats attached to sides. E. Instead of notches, half-round cuts are fitted with shaped brackets (E-1) on which shelves (E-2) rest. Easy way to make strips is to drill a series of holes, then cut on center line (E-3). F. Shelves are drilled to fit on L-shaped hooks. G. Similar to A and E except cuts are triangular. Brackets (G-1) fit into cuts, and shelves (G-2) rest on brackets. For production runs, make V cuts across board (G-3), then cut into individual strips.

. . . or use ready-made hardware

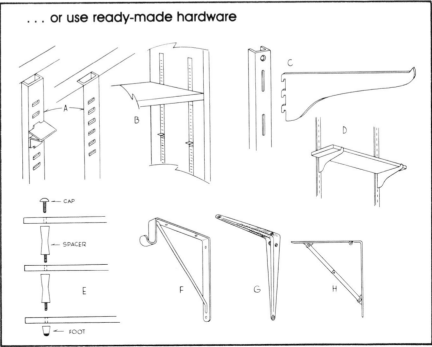

A. Metal wall strip with adjustable clips–can be attached on surface or let into vertical grooves so shelf is flush with sides (B). C. Another type of metal strip, takes shelf brackets–usually used on walls (D). E. Spacers with threaded dowels that fit through holes in shelves allow you to add as many shelves as you have spacers. F. Shelf bracket for closets also holds clothes pole. G. Simple iron shelf bracket for use where appearance is not important. H. Hinged bracket allows shelf, or table, to be folded out of the way.

SELECTING THE RIGHT GLUES AND ADHESIVES

Today there are adhesives for practically every type of fastening job. Some work better in poorly fitted joints, acting as a filler, thereby providing a margin of error for the novice woodworker. Some glues are so waterproof that even boiling water won't loosen their grip.

Some set in seconds to let you hold hard-to-clamp parts together while the glue hardens. Others set over a period of hours to allow time for major assembly work. A few can even be mixed in different proportions to provide different hardening times. There's even one that changes color to signal when hardening has begun. For some types of work you'll have a choice of several adhesives, in which case economy or ease of application may be the deciding factors.

READY-TO-USE TYPES

Aliphatic resin glue. This glue is liquid that resembles heavy cream in color and consistency. It dries translucent with a slight honey tone, and can be precolored with water-soluble dyes to approximate the tone of the wood on which it will be used. It's also nontoxic, nonflammable, and nonstaining.

Though now used by do-it-yourselfers, aliphatic resin glue was originally developed for the furniture industry. Like the traditional "hot" animal glues that required a heated glue pot to keep them at usable consistency, aliphatic glue has high "tack" (instant stickiness) but does not need to be heated. In woodworking projects, this lets you press reinforcements in place (such as concealed glue blocks in drawers) without clamps or other fastenings. Because of the tackiness, the block stays put. But try it first on scrap wood because there can be variations from brand to brand. The glue also has a high degree of moisture resistance, though it's not actually waterproof.

Where clamps are required, they can often be removed in as little as 45 minutes because of the glue's rapid setting time. But keep the work evenly supported overnight before putting it into use. Once set, the glue has high resistance to heat and solvents such as lacquers, varnishes, and sealers—minimizing finishing problems. As the glue sets hard, it sands without gumming and clogging sandpaper. It's a good all-round woodworking and cabinetwork glue—with special advantages in poorly heated workshops because it can be used at temperatures from 45° to 110°F. A high-strength bond can be obtained at low temperature, but longer setting times are needed.

Cellulose nitrate cement. Also called nitrocellulose cement, this has a honey consistency. It is retailed mainly in tubes, although it's available in cans in some brands. The amber-colored cement is useful in two-coat applications, because it shows where the initial coat has been applied. *Caution:* Nitrocellulose cements are flammable.

Application method. On wood where maximum strength is essential, coat both surfaces to be joined. Allow them to dry at least partially before recoating one of the surfaces and pressing the parts together. This procedure allows the cement to penetrate the pores of the wood for a good "bite" and

replaces absorbed cement with the final one-surface coat. In most light work, clamping isn't necessary, but parts should be kept in good contact and in alignment until the cement has set. Where the solvent can evaporate freely, typical cements in this category reach 25 percent of their strength in about two hours—full strength in 24 hours. The holding power is as high as 3,500 pounds per square inch—enough for furniture joints that are small enough for application of this fast-drying cement. The cement will bond a wide variety of porous and nonporous materials. Where the cement is used to bond nonporous materials, the solvent escapes through the edges at the glue line. If a large bonding area

QUICK GUIDE TO GLUES & ADHESIVES

GENERIC & SAMPLE BRAND	TYPE	MATERIALS BONDED	RESISTANCE TO WATER*
Acrylic (P.A.C.)	2-part, liquid & powder	Most porous & nonporous. Make test.	Waterproof
Acrylonitrile (Pliobond)	1-part liquid	Most porous & nonporous. Flexible.	Waterproof
Aliphatic (Titebond)	1-part liquid	Mainly wood & wood products.	Not waterproof
Casein (National Casein Co. No. 30.)	Water-mixed powder	Mainly wood & wood products.	Moisture resistant
Cellulose nitrate (Ambroid)	1-part liquid	Wide range of materials.	Water-resistant
Contact cement (Weldwood Contact Cement)	1-part liquid	Mainly for laminates & veneers to wood or wood products.	Water-resistant
Cyanoacrylate (Krazy Glue)	1-part liquid	Wide range of materials.	Water-resistant
Epoxy (Evercoat Epoxy Glue)	2-parts, both liquid	Wide range of materials.	Waterproof or water-resistant. Fast-set usually has less water resistance.
Hide glue, flake (Cabinetmakers' suppliers)	Water-mixed flakes.	Mainly wood & wood products.	Not waterproof
Hide glue, liquid (Franklin Liquid Hide Glue)	1-part liquid	Mainly wood & wood products.	Not waterproof
Hot-melt glue (Hot-Grip)	1-part solid, liquified by heating	Wide range of materials.	Usually waterproof

is involved, however, considerable time may be required before solvent escapes from the inner area. You can promote more rapid escape by placing a porous material such as a thin layer of wood or fabric between the non-porous materials. Before using this method on important work, experiment on scrap materials.

The relatively low solids content of these cements results in some shrinkage with drying. This tends to draw the parts of a joint together with a fine, sometimes almost invisible glue line. This is an advantage in many types of woodwork. But when large, thin parts are subjected to this shrinkage, distortion can occur, unless some method of bracing is used during the setting period. (Extra-fast-setting types are also available from model builders' suppliers for quick emergency repairs, as at model airplane field competitions.)

Contact cement. This type is available in regular and water-base form, retailed in cans and jars. The regular type is a thin, yellowish syrupy form, based on neoprene and other synthetics with a solvent such as toluol or naptho. *Caution:* This type cement is flammable. Water-based contact cement is of similar consistency but it is usually off-white or milky white in color. Because of its water base, this type of contact cement is nonflammable and can be used where flammable types might be inconvenient or dangerous. For example, it can be used where turning off pilot lights of gas equipment would involve technical know-how. Both types of cement are used in gluing methods not common to other adhesives because contact cements are intended chiefly for the application of thin laminates such as sheet-plastic countertops. One smooth-flowing version is also formulated for wood veneer in cabinetwork.

The usual application procedure requires the use of a heavy paper "slip sheet" as described shortly. To start, both surfaces to be joined are coated with the cement and allowed to dry, which usually takes 30 to 40 minutes. When dry, the regular cement has a glossy sheen. Dull spots indicate inadequate coverage or excessive local absorption, and should be recoated. Water-based cements commonly turn from milky white to light tan when dry. Either can be tested for dryness with a piece of paper. If no cement adheres to a piece of paper pressed lightly against the coated surface, drying is complete, and the cement-coated surfaces are ready to be brought together. Although dry, they will bond instantly on contact. So perfect initial alignment is extremely important.

The "slip sheet" of heavy wrapping paper minimizes the chance of alignment error. Place the paper sheet on the up-facing cement-coated surface, covering the entire area. Then place the cement-coated surface of the laminate downward to rest on the paper. The paper will not stick to either one. Align the laminate precisely, as it is to be on the finished job. Then, holding it carefully in alignment, lift the near edge slightly, and have a helper pull the paper outward an inch or two from under that edge. This allows the two cement-coated surfaces to come together along the area exposed by pulling the paper outward, and holds the laminate in position from then on. (Because only a small area is bonded at the initial stage, it is still possible, though not desirable, to peel off the laminate if it should be misaligned.) If all is well, press down firmly on the area of the laminate under which the paper has been removed. Then withdraw the entire paper. Roll the entire laminate surface down firmly with a small, rubber hand roller from your laminate supplier or from a photo supply store to get a thorough bond. Roll from the center of the laminate toward the edges, working out any raised areas that may indicate trapped air. *Do not rush* this type of work by putting the surfaces together before the cement is dry. Trapped solvent will result in loose areas after the piece has been in use for a while.

Cyanoacrylate adhesive. This type was discovered by accident in the 1950s during basic research on polymers. In the course of routine measurements, scientists found that the prisms of their measuring instrument were adhered inseparably by the sample. Within hours, the scientists determined that the sample also produced strong bonds on a variety of other materials.

Cyanoacrylic adhesives are available in small tubes. Their outstanding characteristic is the quick setting time, measured in seconds. It bonds metals, as well as rubber and most plastics. It is oil and chemical re-

QUICK GUIDE TO GLUES & ADHESIVES

GENERIC & SAMPLE BRAND	TYPE	MATERIALS BONDED	RESISTANCE TO WATER*
Latex combination (Patch-Stix)	1-part liquid	Wide range of materials.	Usually waterproof
Neoprene base (Weldwood Panel & Construction Adhesive)	1-part viscous	Mainly plywood, paneling, etc.	Water-resistant
Polyester (Fibre Glass Evercoat)	2-parts, both liquid. Resin and hardener.	Used mainly on wood, bonding fiberglass.	Waterproof
Polyethylene hot-melt (Thermogrip)	Solid cartridges	Wide range of materials.	Waterproof
Polysulfide (Exide Polysulfide Caulk)	1 and 2-part systems. See text.	Used as caulk and adhesive on wood and other materials.	Waterproof
Polyvinyl acetate. Abbreviated **PVA.** (Fas'n-It)	1-part liquid	Mainly wood, wood products, paper, etc.	Not waterproof
Polyvinyl chloride. Abbreviated **PVC.** (Sheer Magic)	1-part liquid	Wide range of materials.	Water-resistant
Resorcinol resin glue (Weldwood Resorcinol Waterproof Glue)	2-part, liquid & powder	Wood, wood products, plastic laminates, etc.	Waterproof
Rubber base (Black Magic Tough Glue)	1-part viscous	Wide range of materials.	Waterproof
Urea-resin glue (Weldwood Plastic Resin Glue)	Water-mixed powder	Mainly wood and wood products.	Water-resistant
Water-phase epoxy (Dur-A-Poxy)	2-parts, both liquid	Wide range of materials.	Waterproof

*Note: The glues and adhesives in this table are rated as water-resistant or waterproof in relation to their most common uses.

sistant, but it is usually not recommended for parts subject to great shock or peel. And it is not a gap filler. Yet the extremely fast setting time makes the cyanoacrylates well suited to small area repairs where clamping or otherwise supporting the parts is difficult or impossible. Parts can simply be hand-held in position until the joint is firm.

Cyanoacrylates usually carry a warning to avoid inadvertent skin bonding, because these adhesives can stick fingers together or to other objects almost instantly. If this happens, powerful pull-apart methods are *not* recommended. Devcon recommends placing the affected parts under running water and working a small rounded object such as a paper clip gently between them to separate them. Bond-Solv available from Edmund Scientific Company offers another means of separating. This is a special solvent formulated to separate parts bonded by certain cyanoacrylates. For separating, the safest bet is to follow the manufacturer's instructions implicitly.

Hide glue (liquid). This is a modern liquid form of the traditional cabinetmaker glue. Unlike the flake forms of hide glue, the liquid form is ready to use as it comes from the container; it requires no heating. Liquid hide glue has a moderately long setting time that allows precise, unhurried assembly of parts without risk of ''chilled'' joints sometimes encountered with ''hot'' glues. Heat resistant and unaffected by most lacquers, varnish, and sealers, it's a good, home-shop glue.

Polyvinyl acetate glue (PVA). Often simply called ''white glue,'' this is a polyvinyl-acetate-resin emulsion usually retailed in plastic squeeze bottles of many sizes. Although milk white in liquid state, most brands dry colorless and transparent, forming an almost invisible glue line. PVA is a good glue for cabinetwork but should not be used in joints that are under sustained load where the glue alone must resist the load. (Most furniture joints themselves are designed to provide structural support for sustained loads; the glue merely holds the joint together.) Nor should PVA be subjected to high humidity and high temperature, because both tend to reduce PVA's gripping power. Yet under normal conditions, PVA has high strength and impact resistance.

For application, spread PVA over both surfaces to be joined. Most brands should not be left more than 10 minutes before you join the parts. Corrosion will result if you use PVA on metal or place it in metal containers.

WATER-MIXED TYPES

Casein glue. This is made from a protein precipitated from skim milk. In its usual form, the glue is a light-tan powder, usually in cans, that must be mixed with water. Casein glue is an easy-to-use and inexpensive gap-filler type adhesive that can be used at any shop temperature above freezing. Although not waterproof, it is highly water resistant, having retained its bond strength for more than a quarter century in weather-protected joints in the framework of covered bridges. It is also resistant to grease, oil, and gasoline. Casein glue is well suited to most home wood-working projects and is especially good for gluing resinous or oily woods. It is widely used, too, in gluing laminated work, particularly on large jobs such as rafters, where its low cost is important.

Mixing instructions for some brands give the proportions of glue powder and water by volume, typically 1 part glue powder to 1 part water. Others give proportions by weight, typically 1 pound of glue powder to 2 pounds of water. Be sure to add glue to water (not the other way around) and stir rapidly until the powder absorbs the water and becomes thick and pasty. Let this thick mixture stand for 10 to 15 minutes but *do not add water*. During this standing period the water dissolves the powdered glue. Stir again after this, and the thick pasty mix smooths out like heavy cream and is ready to apply. As a general rule clamps should be used for at least the first 4 to 5 hours of drying time. At 70°F, a hardening time of about 8 hours completes the job, though humid air may slow it. If you want to double-check on full hardening, start a test joint of scrap wood at the same time as the work itself, and break-test it after overnight drying. (Test joints are a good precaution in any critical work with any glue.)

Hide glue (flake). This is the traditional ''hot glue'' (readied in heated pots) by cabinetmakers. It is still available by the pound in flake form from cabinetwork supply houses. Although not waterproof, and subject to weakening by dampness, hide glue is well suited to fine cabinetwork not exposed to excessive moisture. It is practically nonstaining and has a shear strength of a ton per square inch. The usual preparation procedure consists of soaking the flakes in water to soften them, then heating with a prescribed amount of water to produce the final hot mix. (Obtain specific instructions for the brand you buy from the dealer.) The glue should be applied to the work while still hot to avoid ''chilled'' joints that can't be properly assembled because the glue cools and stiffens before assembly. Electric glue pots that heat the glue to the proper temperature and maintain it at that temperature are usually available from glue suppliers.

Urea-resin glue. Now widely termed plastic-resin glue, this is commonly sold as a light-tan powder packaged in cans of various sizes for home-shop use. It is prepared for use by mixing with water. Typical proportions by volume are 5 parts resin to 2 parts water. The mixing method usually calls for mixing the glue powder with enough water to make a thick paste, stirring continuously. Then the remainder of the water is added to bring the mix to the consistency of heavy cream, again with continuous stirring. If any small lumps remain, stirring is continued to dissolve them. When smooth, the glue is ready for use.

This is a good cabinetwork glue because it is nonstaining, highly water resistant, and stronger than most wood. Also, it is unaffected by oil, gasoline, and common finish solvents. It is *not* a gap filler type glue, however, and requires well-fitted joints and clamping to assure tight glue lines. (In wide gaps it tends to crystalize and crumble with time. In tightly fitted joints it does not.) As a rule, clamps should remain in place 3 to 6 hours on softwoods, 5 to 7 hours on hardwoods, at around 70°F. At higher temperatures the clamping time can be reduced. On work where appearance is not important, nails may be used in place of clamps. The glue should be spread on both meeting surfaces in a thin coat, and then assembled and clamped while still moist.

HOT-MELT GLUES

Multi-resin hot-melt glue. Like Hot-Grip, this glue is formulated for a variety of gluing applications. It is especially suited to the bonding of plastics, such as polyethylene and polypropylene, that cannot be bonded by ordinary adhesives. The hot-melt glue will bond plastics to each other or to other materials such as vinyl, metal, and wood. To ensure a firm bond, the adhesive contains a combination of resins in a formula that liquifies when heated, makes its bond in the liquid state, then solidifies on cooling.

Hot-Grip resembles butterscotch in color and is packaged in metal pans in which it may be heated for use. Since it hardens by cooling, not by the evaporation of a solvent, it can be used to bond nonporous materials such as glazed tile and steel. *Note:* This works only if you apply the glue and complete the assembly before the glue cools. In all applications the work must be planned, and the parts readied to permit assembly immediately after the glue is applied. If assembly is delayed, the glue may cool and harden before the joint can be made. The glue may also be used to lock splices in polyethylene and polypropylene rope used for towing water skiers and for other marine activities.

Polyethylene-based hot-melt glue. This is commonly sold in cartridges that must be used with an electric glue gun designed for them. The glue sticks to most materials. It is waterproof, moderately flexible, and very fast setting — forming a bond ready for handling in about a minute. It is light-cream in color before and after application.

To apply the glue, plug in the gun and allow it to preheat (time may vary with brand). Then insert the glue cartridge, place the point of the gun muzzle on the surface to be glued, and feed the cartridge into the gun with thumb pressure or by trigger action if the gun has a trigger feed. Move the muzzle along the gluing line quickly to permit assembly before the glue cools. Apply the glue to only one of the joining surfaces. Press the other surface of the joint against the glued surface within 20 seconds of application so the glue will not cool before assembly. Hold the parts in position for another 20 seconds, after which they will hold their position. The glue develops 90 percent of its full strength in 60 seconds, the remaining 10 percent in 24 hours. Because of its rapid setting, it is excellent for quick repairs and for work where the parts can be joined progressively, as in gluing gimp to furniture in upholstery work. It is also suited to caulking and seam filling. It should not, of course, be used on jobs requiring application over large areas that might cool before the parts can be assembled. In all work, the glue is simply applied as a bead, just as it comes from the gun. It is *not* spread by spatula or other means. Spreading takes place naturally when the gluing surfaces are pressed together.

TWO-PART ADHESIVES

Acrylic resin glue. This is packaged in two parts, one a powder, the other a liquid. It sticks to almost any material and is one of the strongest and fastest setting of all adhesives. Of the generally available types, only hot-melt forms and cyanoacrylates set faster. Acrylic resin glue is also one of the highest-priced adhesives, however. Twin-container packages range in size from 4 ounces to 1 gallon. (Special forms of the resin are available for dental work.)

The glue is exceptional for special marine uses, especially those for which other marine glues are unsuitable. But the rapid (5-minute) setting time generally limits it to jobs that can be coated and assembled quickly. Since the full curing time for some mixes is as long as 30 minutes, these glues can be used for longer periods than many others. The safest procedure is to mix a small test batch and try it for spreadability at 30-second intervals until it becomes unworkable. The manufacturer's instructions will indicate the proportion that provides the longest and shortest working times. One brand, P.A.C., changes color from white to distinct yellow when the mix is no longer workable.

The glue can be used to repair a broken spar when the angle of the break is long enough to make repair feasible. In this case, the broken ends are fitted together dry, then moved apart about $\frac{3}{16}$ inch. After the bottom of the opening is sealed with self-adhering tape, a thin liquid mix is then poured into the gap. The parts are then moved together. No clamping is necessary unless for alignment. This method is designed to coat a relatively large and complex gluing surface in the shortest possible time. The temperature of the workroom may be relatively low because the mix generates its own heat. Before using the method above, check the manufacturer's instructions.

Since the glue has unlimited gap-filling ability, it fills gaps left by split-off fragments. It can even be used to fill large holes. As to strength, at least one large sailing ship has sailed around the world with a spar that had been repaired with acrylic adhesive.

In normal wood gluing the surfaces to be joined are sometimes given a quick pre-brushing with the pure liquid component prior to applying the mixed adhesive; this increases penetration. Whatever the material being glued, the meeting surfaces should be thoroughly clean and slightly roughened if possible. Once set, the glue is completely waterproof and unaffected by oil, gas, and many common solvents. Tools and containers can be cleaned with such solvents, however, while the glue is still wet. Hardening is so rapid that disposable containers and applicators are advisable.

Epoxy glue. This is a two-part glue consisting of a liquid resin and a liquid hardener. Because formulas vary, the parts must be mixed in the proportions specified by the manufacturer. When packaged in tubes, the two parts of the epoxy glue are usually formulated to produce a stiff consistency and to harden properly when mixed in a 1-to-1 proportion. Typical package sizes range from as little as 30 cc in tubes, to gallon cans for marine use. Owing to the honey consistency of the unmixed resin in can sizes, it is often thinned slightly with additives to ease spreading.

If the resin is to be used between nonporous materials, however, it should be "100 percent solids," which means that it consists only of the resin and its hardener, with no solvents or thinners that must evaporate before mating of the surfaces. Then, when mixed, the entire quantity of both liquid components solidifies. Since nothing is lost from the mixture, it can harden without evaporation, and it does not shrink. The usual color of the pure resin ranges from clear to honey, unless colored for mixing purposes.

Surfaces to be joined should be thoroughly cleaned and slightly roughened, if possible. The glue should be applied to both meeting surfaces. Because of the toughness of the hardened glue, squeeze-out should be removed from the work with an acetone-dampened cloth before the glue hardens. This reduces the amount of sanding required later.

Working time and curing time varies with the particular adhesive. In a typical instance, you can figure on a working time of about 2 hours, a tack-free drying time of about 3 hours, and a complete cure in about 18 hours at 70°F. Some formulas differ very widely from these figures. So follow the guides supplied with the one you use. Though very slow-setting epoxies take a week to harden, some brands can be painted or finished as soon as the glue is tack-free. But check labels.

Once set, epoxy is completely waterproof and unaffected by most common solvents and many acids. It can be removed from tools with acetone while still liquid. But since the job is slow, you'll be wiser to use disposable brushes, applicators, and mixing containers.

You can use epoxy on almost any material, including wood, to provide a permanent bond of unusually high strength. In wood gluing, however, other glues (such as resorcinol, described in the following section) can provide practically the same or better qualities and strength, often at lower cost. So, unless special problems are involved, they provide sensible economy.

Resorcinol resin glue. This is packaged in twin cans, one containing the syrupy, burgundy-colored resin, the other the powdered catalyst. The two components are usually mixed in the proportions of 4 liquid to 3 powdered catalyst. Thinning may be done when necessary with a very small amount of alcohol or water. The twin container sizes range from quarter-pint to gallon size at retail outlets.

Before hardening, resorcinol glue can be washed easily from tools and containers, using plain water. After hardening, it is completely waterproof and unaffected by water, gasoline, oil, mild acids, alkalis, or common solvents. Even prolonged boiling does not weaken it. Resorcinol is a leading boat-building glue, stronger than wood at temperatures from minus 40°F to temperatures high enough to set the wood afire. Hardening time varies from 10 hours at 70°F (the minimum safe working temperature) to 3 hours at 100°F. It can be sanded and painted as soon as it is hard, though it continues to gain strength for several weeks. It is a moderately good gap-filler glue and can be held together either by clamping or by nails or screws. The fastenings may be left in place or removed after the glue sets. You can judge the hardness of the glue by feeling droplets of squeeze-out. When they "click" off, the bond is strong enough to be put in service. The working life of the mixed glue is about 3 hours at 70°F. But to play safe, plan your work to be completed in a somewhat shorter period. Here, working time can be shortened by temperature variations and sunlight. In hot weather you can extend the working time (or maintain the 70°F figure)

by setting the glue container in a bowl of cracked ice. When mixing, be especially careful to avoid inhaling the powdered catalyst or allowing it to get into your eyes, for it is caustic. The powder tends to pack during storage. So before mixing the two components, shake the closed can of powdered catalyst vigorously to "fluff" it. This ensures that the measured proportions will be accurate. *Important:* Use a *separate* measuring implement for the two parts, and

be *very careful* not to allow any of the powdered catalyst to get into the can of unused resin. Even a slight amount of the powder in the unused resin can gradually stiffen it and make it unfit for use. Wash all mixing measures thoroughly after use to prevent inadvertent contamination of subsequent batches. The glue is chemically related to that used in waterproof plywood, and is comparable in performance. It was developed originally for use in torpedo-boat construction.

WOOD GLUING METHODS

Properly used, most modern wood glues are stronger than the wood you're likely to use them on. But your gluing methods and the temperature of the work area are major factors in attaining that strength. Since there's often a variation between brands of a given glue, and even between different versions of the same basic type made by the same manufacturer, your first step should be to read the manufacturer's instructions.

TERMINOLOGY OF GLUE TIMING

Gluing instructions for major jobs usually include a timetable covering several different working temperatures. The first item on the timetable usually is the pot life, or working life, of the glue, which is the time (usually in hours) the glue remains usable after it has been prepared. The second item on the timetable is the maximum open assembly time. This, usually in minutes, is the period after the glue has been applied, before the parts must be brought together. Next, is the *maximum* "closed" assembly time—the period after the parts are brought together, but before clamping pressure is applied. The final item is the *minimum* curing period (usually in hours) required before the glued object can be handled. Some instructions specify the pressure period required, as well as the type of handling and finishing work that may be done immediately afterward. Although these timetables vary with the brand, the sample timetable that follows is typical for plastic resin glues.

Temperature (°F)	70	80	90
Pot life (hours)	4–5	2½–3½	1–2
Maximum assembly times			
Open (minutes)	15	10	5
Closed (minutes)	25	15	8
Pressure period (hours)	12	8	5

Note: Assembly time for ready-to-use aliphatic and PVA (white) is about 5 minutes open, 15 minutes closed.

Following the pressure period or minimum curing time, most wood glues continue to gain strength during a "maturing period," which can be a considerable length of time. A typical resorcinol, for example, reaches *ultimate* strength and waterproofness in about 6 days at room temperature. But you can usually begin machining, shaping, and finishing on the project after an 8- to 24-hour period. To gauge the glue's degree of hardness, make a sample joint of scrap wood at the same time as you glue the project, and allow a little excess squeeze-out so you can test hardness. Of course, at higher room temperatures, the tempering period is reduced.

In general, there's no need to rush the assembly if you remain within the maximums specified by the manufacturer. Instructions for glues such as casein, plastic resin, and resorcinol, in fact, may specify a minimum assembly time as well as maximum. The minimum assures that the glue will have time to penetrate the wood pores (to assure bond strength) and to thicken slightly without surface-drying before application of pressure. If no minimum assembly time is given, and you're working with very dense wood or nonporous material, you can keep the joints open during a major part of the *maximum open* assembly time. With resorcinol, this might be 3 minutes. But watch it, because the drying rate of a glue depends on variables such as air humidity, absorbency of the wood, and the wood's moisture content. Don't allow the glue to become overly tacky or to "skin over" before you bring the parts together. If the instructions do not include the information you need, contact the manufacturer for further details. Manufacturers often have special literature for guidance on jobs in which peak glue performance is critical.

SOLVING AIR TEMPERATURE PROBLEMS

Temperature in the work area is more likely to be a problem in winter than in summer. If you can keep your workroom at 70°F or more, you can use any type of glue. If you can't maintain 70°F temperatures, you can either select a glue that will harden at the expected temperature, or use some form of auxiliary heat during the gluing and harden-

ing periods. Low-temperature cabinetwork glues include casein (such as National Casein Company's No. 30), which hardens at any temperature above freezing, and aliphatic resin glue (such as Franklin Glue Company's Titebond), which can be used at temperatures from 45°F up to 110°. White glues usually require a minimum 50° temperature. Nitrocellulose cements, such as Ambroid, set by evaporation rather than chemical action and so can be used at temperatures below freezing (though sub-zero cementing isn't recommended). Ambroid cements are limited to smaller gluing areas than casein and the aliphatics because of their quick-drying qualities. At low temperatures, the clamping and curing times of all glues are much greater. For example, at 40°F a typical casein glue would require about 20 hours clamping time and another 96 hours curing time to develop handling strength. At 80°F, clamping time for the same glue could be shortened to about 2 hours, with about 24 hours curing time. If you're using casein, do your mixing in a warm area (not with warm water) in order to assure that the glue is completely dissolved before use. (Do not mix casein in an aluminum container.) With nitrocellulose cements, try to apply the cement in a warm place. The work may then be cured in a colder area. If the cement is applied in a very cold area, increased viscosity caused by the low temperature may make it difficult to spread. Since low-temperature gluing introduces time-related variables such as increased time for evaporation and absorption, you may prefer to avoid complications by using auxiliary heat. When using auxiliary heat for your work area, be sure the wood you'll be gluing is at the same temperature as the heated room. If it's stored in an unheated area, bring it into the heated area at least a day in advance. Be sure to separate the pieces so the heated air can reach all surfaces. Cold wood, even in a heated room, can chill the glue below its required hardening temperature and in many cases, keep it chilled long enough to adversely affect joint strength. To play safe, be sure both the room and the materials are at the required temperature.

PLANNING AND DRY RUNS

Large gluing jobs, as in boatbuilding and major cabinetwork, require advance planning to divide the work into stages that can be done within the glue's time limits. You should also avoid gluing an assembly in such a way that a final part can't be put in place without disturbing glued parts. In some cases, too, only one order of assembly is possible. The best way to dodge problems is by making a dry run, without glue.

GLUE APPLICATION

On small jobs with glue that's difficult to clean from a brush, it's often wise to use an easily cleaned spatula, a disposable wooden paddle, or a pointed stick, depending on the job. In model work with white glue or cellulose cement, wood paddles and pointed sticks can be reused many times without cleaning. Just whittle off the hardened adhesive. For major home-shop gluing jobs, of course, the paint brush is the commonest application tool. Use a cheap disposable brush for hard-to-remove glue, such as epoxy. Select a width that matches as closely as possible the width of the coating required. For example,

use a ¾-inch width brush for a ¾-inch board edge. Apply the glue as you would apply paint, and if the brush is to be cleaned, do the cleaning as soon as possible after applying the glue. If the parts to be joined are well matched so that full surface contact is assured, coat only one of the two meeting surfaces. If the surfaces are long or varied in contour, as in boat-building, coat both surfaces. The same applies to any surfaces where the fit is at all doubtful.

In cabinet and boat work, apply enough glue so a *slight* squeeze-out shows along the glue line where the parts are clamped. You may want to make a few trial joints with scrap wood. Remember, you don't want so much squeeze-out that it runs down the wood surface. (You can wipe it off, but you're wasting glue, and some types may cause staining.) If you want to give the wood an unpainted natural or stained finish, remove squeeze-out very carefully. You can do this with a cloth dampened with the glue solvent (water for water mixed glues) while the glue is still fresh. You can also let the glue set to a rubbery consistency and shave off the squeeze-out in a long, thin strip by sliding a sharp chisel along it. This must be done

before the glue is really hard. Once the squeeze-out is hard, removal requires sanding. For natural finishing, a certain amount of fine sanding is usually required, even though you remove the squeeze-out by wiping with a damp cloth or by shaving with a chisel. The fine sanding removes any minute squeeze-out leftovers, smooths raised grain, and takes off possible remaining glue film that might cause uneven tones during staining and finishing.

FILLING GAPS

If minor gaps appear in poorly fitted joints, they can be filled with wood filler after the glue hardens. If the gaps are likely to weaken the bond significantly, fill them with a glue-coated wood sliver, while the glue is still wet. If you don't discover the gap until the glue has hardened, you can still use the sliver, bonded in place with epoxy. Most epoxies are good gap fillers and will bond to almost anything, including the hardened glue in a misfitted joint. To speed this type of error-patch, you can also use an acrylic adhesive, which can harden in as little as 5 minutes if mixed for fast setting.

PROTECTING THE WOOD

Glue that's allowed to soak into the wood is likely to require considerable additional effort if you want to avoid an uneven finish tone, especially if the work is to be stained. Even clear-drying glue can cause an uneven finish because it seals wood pores that would otherwise absorb the finishing stain.

Aside from wiping, there are several other ways to protect your project from squeeze-out trouble. One of the simplest is to use the correct amount of glue for minimum squeeze-out. You can gauge this in advance

by testing the glue with scrap wood and clamps. (There should be a slight squeeze-out.) You can also protect the work with cellulose or vinyl tape on the low side of the glue line, or on both sides if the seam is vertical. Apply the tape before gluing, of course, and be sure it's firmly bonded, especially close to the glue line. If it isn't, there's a chance the glue may work under it by capillary action. You can use the tip of a teaspoon to press the tape down for a tight seal. Another method calls for the application of

finish coats to seal the exterior of the work before applying glue to the mating surfaces. This prevents soak-in of squeeze-out. Allow the finish to dry before gluing the parts together. Of course, the finish must be one that will not be affected by the glue. In addition, always have a container of glue solvent at hand to clean squeeze-out from the tape.

For most woodworking glues the solvent (before hardening) is water, so it can be in an open top container such as a jelly glass for easy dipping of your wiping cloth. The cloth should be moist but not wet, because you don't want water or other solvent to soak into the glue line.

CLAMPS

Few of the projects you make would hang together for long if it were not for the fact that clamps can be used to hold the parts until the adhesive dries. Nails and screws and fastening hardware can be used, of course, but this is not always practical or compatible with quality craftsmanship. So—clamps are in order.

There are different types of clamps; so many, in fact, that it can be discouraging because each type does a particular job especially well and a large assortment of clamps can run into money. But don't despair, because a basic assortment can take

you a long way. You can "make do" with clamps you already have, you can add to your set by making your own, and you can improvise along some of the lines shown in the photos.

Even if money is in great supply it's not wise to buy clamps just to fill a cabinet, because it *is* possible to buy types that you will never really have use for or which you will require so infrequently you'd be better off improvising on those occasions.

Do become familar with different types so you can choose your first purchases in line with the majority of jobs you will be doing

regularly. There are many types of bar clamps, some made with fixtures that can't be removed so the length of span is limited by the length of the bar. It may be better to buy fixtures which can be used on ordinary galvanized pipe. Thus, with several sets of fixtures and an assortment of pipe lengths, you can suit the clamp to the job.

You can exert great pressure with a clamp so don't use more than hand-pressure to tighten them. Pounding with a hammer or increasing leverage by using a length of pipe on the handle is forbidden. If you don't damage or bend the clamp itself you will certainly mar the work. If excessive pressure is needed to draw parts together it is wise to assume that the pieces do not fit.

CLAMPING TIPS:

1. Preparation of the surfaces to be bonded is important since neglect here can cause a weak joint. Mating areas should be thoroughly dusted. Hard, dense surfaces will glue better if they are roughened slightly by some sanding across the grain.

2. Apply glue carefully to avoid staining adjacent surfaces. Glue squeezed out of a joint under clamping pressure should be wiped off immediately with a damp cloth. If the glue is allowed to remain, it will seal the wood and prevent stain penetration. If you allow it to dry, you'll have a rough sanding job on hand.

3. Glue does have body, which is one reason why joints should not fit so tightly they must be forced into place. This is especially true of fittings like the mortise-tenon and dowel joints. The ends of tenons should be chamfered to allow some room for excess glue. Dowels should be grooved or you can buy the ready-made type which are spiraled. Thus when the dowel is pushed into the hole, the groove, or the spiral, permits the escape of excess glue and air. A tight-fitting dowel joint can force glue out elsewhere or can create pressure that will split the stock.

4. Some woods like lemonwood, teak, even varieties of pine can contain oil or pitch. This will leave a surface film that will prevent a good gluing job. Sometimes the bond appears to hold—until you put some pressure on it. Then it parts as if you had used saliva instead of glue. In cases like this, clean the surfaces carefully and use a casein glue.

5. Never use anything but your fingers to tighten clamps. Excessive pressure can squeeze out too much of the glue. You don't want to clamp so lightly that you get no

Here is an example of how a set of hinged bar clamps can be attached to a bench surface to create a jig. Similar assemblies can pass through and be held firmly for either nailing or gluing.

Glue-coated edges should be pulled up tight enough so a thin bead of glue is squeezed out along each joint line. Too much pressure will merely remove more of the glue and "starve" the joint. Note the homemade clamping fixture.

Wooden pony-bar cabinet clamps are used on fine work where a lot of pressure is not required. As the wooden bar is unlikely to harm finished surfaces, this type of clamp is used widely for exacting repair work.

C-clamps are made in various sizes and can be quite useful in woodworking. Be sure to use scrap pieces to protect the work.

Notched-bar clamps are simple and easy to use. They can be purchased in size ranging in opening capacity from 2' to 8'.

This type of press screw (left) may be attached anywhere to solve a clamping problem, or to create a jig for repeat clamping of similar assemblies to speed the work. Two kinds of hand-screws are available; the adjustable type (right) permits the jaws to be set at various angles to suit the work; the nonadjustable type (not shown) has jaws which remain practically parallel.

"squeeze-out." If clamping pressure is okay and no glue is squeezed out, it is a good sign that you haven't applied enough glue or that there is a gap or chamber where the glue can collect.

6. Most times, and this is especially true of porous materials, both mating surfaces should be glue-coated. To some extent this will depend on the product being used so this is another valid reason for reading labels and following directions.

There are "filler-type" glues; these have sufficient body or a particular additive that enables them to compensate somewhat for a poor fit. Usually, a heavy application to both surfaces is advised with some free drying time before the parts are mated but, again, follow the manufacturer's instructions.

7. Most glues are best applied by brush since this permits full and uniform application. On broad surfaces you can get good coverage by using a toothed spreader. One good trick for many uses is to thread a length of ½" rope through a short piece of tubing until it projects about 1" from one end. Unravel this end and use it to spread glue. To renew the end, all you have to do is snip off the used portion and pull out another inch of the rope.

8. Never put a joint under stress until you have allowed sufficient drying time. Some glues will set faster than others but few are ready to take strain immediately. Setting time can sometimes be pushed but never in a way that ignores instructions. The setting time of urea-resin glue can be speeded up by applying heat to the joint. For some projects a heat-lamp is practical. Glue should not be applied to very cold surfaces nor should the glue be cold; it should run freely.

These are fixed-head I-beam bar clamps and pipe clamps which are made by buying the fixtures and using them on ordinary pipes to make a clamp of any length.

Improvised setup for clamping irregular work. The "clamp" consists of two hardwood bars, two nuts and bolts and a couple of lengths of line.

Another improvised setup that facilitates a tough gluing job. Scrap blocks are placed against the legs after being drilled to permit passage of the line. A turnbuckle pulls the line taut; tapping down on the blocks presses the legs squarely against the post.

These clamps have spring-operated jaws which can be used to hold almost any material. Fast to use, they are fine for holding parts temporarily while you secure them or even for small glue jobs.

Curved components can be shaped by laminating thin strips which are easily bent. The clamping fixture has matching, curved blocks which are preshaped to the line required. Taking up on the wing nut shapes the pieces and holds them together until the glue sets.

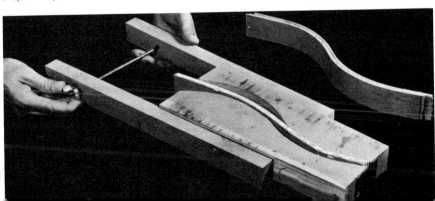

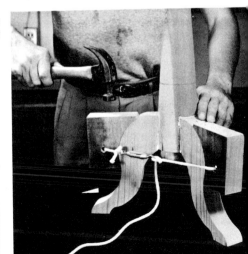

SCREWS AND NAILS

When correctly driven, screws have great holding power and, of importance in many applications, they can be removed if necessary. Another consideration of importance in furniture construction is that they pull parts together. Not only does this add to strength and rigidity but in some instances it can eliminate the need for clamping. Screws can be more decorative than nails and in many applications are more acceptable exposed than nails would be.

Unless you are working with very small screws, or the material is quite soft, it is a wise procedure to drill a pilot hole to eliminate splitting and make screw-driving easier. The depth and diameter of the pilot hole are quite important since they should permit the screw to drive easily, yet not open the material to the point where the screw loses efficiency. The shank, or body hole, is always the same size—or maybe a fraction larger—than the gauge of the screw. When used, a countersink should have a diameter and a bevel angle to match the screwhead. On soft materials, the depth of the countersink can be less than needed since taking up on the screw will sink it enough so it will be flush with adjacent surfaces. It is also true that small screws in hard woods and screws up to an inch long and as heavy as 5 gauge in soft woods can be driven very satisfactorily by using an awl or an icepick to form a starting hole. Never get a screw started by driving it part way with a hammer.

A fairly typical procedure that you might follow when using screws to hold two boards together would be as follows:

Hold the boards together under clamps or tack-nail if possible. Then lay out the screw locations. Drill the pilot hole through the first piece of wood and into the second. Enlarge the pilot hole in the first piece of

MATCHING SCREWS AND DRILL SIZES FOR PILOT AND CLEARANCE HOLES

Screw	Pilot Holes				Clearance Holes	
	HARDWOODS		SOFTWOODS			
	A	B	A	B	A	B
0	1/32"	66	1/64"	75	1/16"	52
1		57	1/32	71	5/64	47
2		54	1/32	65	3/32	42
3	1/16	53	3/64	58	7/64	37
4	1/16	51	3/64	55	7/64	32
5	5/64	47	1/16	53	1/8	30
6		44	1/16	52	9/64	27
7		39	1/16	51	5/32	22
8	7/64	35	5/64	48	11/64	18
9	7/64	33	5/64	45	3/16	14
10	1/8	31	3/32	43	3/16	10
11		29	3/32	40	13/32	4
12		25	7/64	38	7/32	2
14	3/16	14	7/64	32	1/4	D
16		10	9/64	29	17/64	I
18	13/64	6	9/64	26	19/64	N
20	7/32	3	11/64	19	21/64	P
24	1/4	D	3/16	15	3/8	V

NOTE:

A = Closest size twist drill (in fractions of an inch)
B = Number or letter size drill

FLAT HEAD ROUND HEAD OVAL HEAD

LENGTH

PHILLIPS HEAD

FLAT HEAD ROUND HEAD OVAL HEAD

Wood screws come with flat, round, or oval heads. Flat-headed screws are usually countersunk, round- or oval-headed screws either left exposed or counterbored. Slotted screws are driven with a regular screwdriver; Phillips head screws require special Phillips screwdriver.

Actual sizes of heads and shanks.

Head

Shank

No. 24   No. 20   No. 18   No. 16   No. 14   No. 12   No. 11

No. 10   No. 9   No. 8   No. 7   No. 6   No. 5   No. 4   No. 3   No. 2   No. 1   No. 0

Actual head and shank sizes of wood screws No. 0 through No. 24. Lengths vary from 1/4" to 5" depending on size.

wood to the shank size of the screw and then, if needed, form the countersink. It's easy to see what happens when you drive the screw. It begins to grip as it enters the second piece of wood and, during the last turn or two, it pulls the first piece down tightly against the second one.

Screwdrivers come in various sizes so it's a good idea to have an assortment on hand so you can match the blade of the screwdriver to the size of the screw. It should fit the slot in the screw-head snugly and its width at the tip should not be greater than the diameter of the screw-head. This works out quite logically since screwdrivers with broad, heavy tips will have longer and heavier handles so driving large screws will be easier. On the other hand, the smaller screws require more delicate screwdrivers, which makes it difficult to apply so much pressure that you run the danger of ruining the slot and even snapping the screw.

When driving a screw is difficult, even when the lead hole is correct (and this will

happen in some materials), try coating the threads with soap or wax. This will make them drive more easily. If you make a mistake and drill an oversize lead hole, or if repeated removals have enlarged the hole to the point where the screw threads no longer grip tightly, you can often compensate by partially filling the hole with some steel wool or small slivers of wood. If these or similar methods don't do the trick, then change to the next size screw.

Screws can be concealed by countersinking deeper than necessary and then filling the hole with wood dough. This, however, is not the most satisfactory method. A better way is to counterbore deep enough so the screw-head will end up about ¼″ below the wood surface. Then fill the hole with a dowel. This can be sanded flush after the glue dries. If you plan much of this, it will be wise to check into getting a few plug cutters. With these you can make your own short dowels from the same material used in the project, which will make it possible to match the con-

cealment plug to surrounding areas to the point where it will be difficult to discern.

Screws come in many materials—brass, steel, stainless steel, aluminum, galvanized or plated with chromium or cadmium, and there are screws with decorative heads. Usually, when you buy a piece of decorator hardware, you will get screws with it that will match the finish and the design of the piece.

Except for the attachment of hardware or detail components which can't be secured in other ways, most screws in furniture construction are hidden, so steel or galvanized steel screws work out quite well.

DOS AND DON'TS OF NAILS AND NAILING

Select nails on the basis of appearance and length. If holding power is more important than appearance, use common nails. When appearance is more important, select finishing nails since they can be set beneath the surface of the wood so they are hidden. Nail length is based on application. Generally speaking, the nail length should be three times the thickness of the face piece. For example, if you were nailing through the surface of 1″ stock to attach the piece to the edge of another, the nail should be 3″ long. When face-nailing two pieces (surface-to-

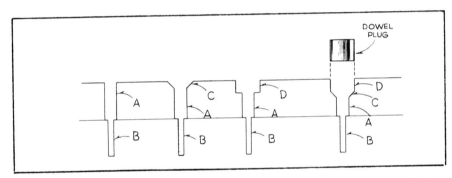

Correct method of joining two pieces of wood with screws: First, drill pilot hole (B) through both pieces. Second, drill shank, or clearance, hole (A) through top piece. Third, countersink hole if screw head is to be flush with surface. If dowel plugs are used to conceal screws, drill hole for plug (D) first. Pilot hole should be half the length of threaded portion of screw.

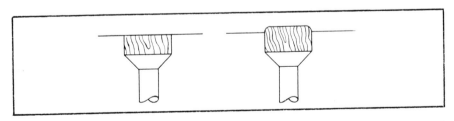

Dowel plugs may be sanded flush or allowed to project as a decorative detail. Plugs may also be made from a contrasting wood.

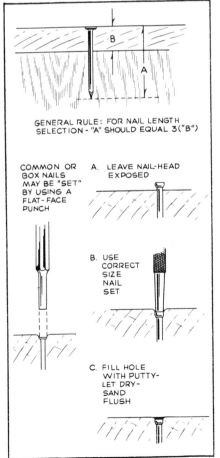

GENERAL RULE: FOR NAIL LENGTH SELECTION - "A" SHOULD EQUAL 3("B")

COMMON OR BOX NAILS MAY BE "SET" BY USING A FLAT-FACE PUNCH

A. LEAVE NAIL-HEAD EXPOSED

B. USE CORRECT SIZE NAIL SET

C. FILL HOLE WITH PUTTY-LET DRY-SAND FLUSH

RECOMMENDED SCREWS FOR PLYWOOD

Plywood Thickness	Flat-Head Screws		
	screw	length	pilot hole
$\frac{3}{4}''$	#8	$1\frac{1}{2}''$	$\frac{5}{32}''$
$\frac{5}{8}$	#8	$1\frac{1}{4}$	$\frac{5}{32}$
$\frac{1}{2}$	#6	$1\frac{1}{4}$	$\frac{1}{8}$
$\frac{3}{8}$	#6	1	$\frac{1}{8}$
$\frac{1}{4}$	#4	$\frac{3}{4}$	$\frac{7}{64}$

surface) select a nail length that will be about ³⁄₁₆″ or ¼″ less than the combined thickness of the two pieces.

When working with finishing nails, hammer-drive the nail until the nail head is *almost* flush. Then use a nail set to finish the job. Use the right nail set; they come in sizes that range from ¹⁄₃₂″ up to ⁵⁄₃₂″. Since they are not expensive, it's wise to buy a set rather than a single unit. Don't set nails deeper than ¹⁄₁₆″ to ⅛″.

End or edge nailing requires special care, especially when the wood has a tendency to split. Sometimes, blunting the nail by tapping the point with the hammer helps. If it doesn't, then drill small holes before driving the nails.

A lot of nails driven on the same line will almost surely split the wood. Fewer nails and staggered will spread the strain over more grain lines, will be stronger and will minimize the possibility of splitting. If a nail bends you can sometimes continue driving it if you use pliers to straighten it *at the bend*. Don't force it if it continues to bend; remove it and use another.

Use light hammer blows to start a nail and be especially careful to start it straight. Heavy grain will sometimes deflect a nail point and send it off in another direction to emerge where it's least wanted. If experience with a first few tries indicates this is likely, then take the time and trouble to drill small holes first.

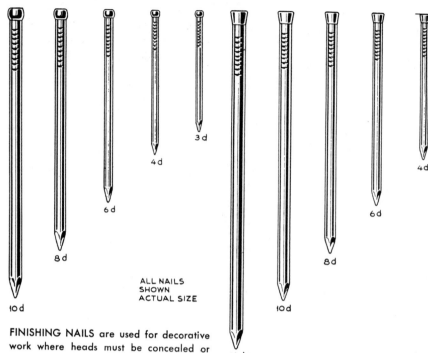

ALL NAILS SHOWN ACTUAL SIZE

FINISHING NAILS are used for decorative work where heads must be concealed or flush with work surface. Some have cupped heads which make them easier to counter-sink and cover with wood putty.

CASING NAILS are used for interior trim and cabinet work. They are slightly heavier in gauge than finishing nails but are otherwise similar.

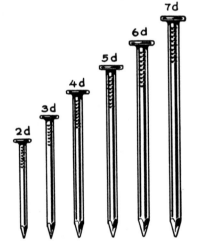

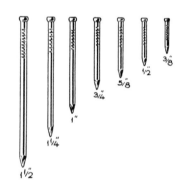

COMMON NAILS are made for general construction work where nail heads do not have to be concealed, although they can be "set" with a flat-faced punch. They come as large as 60d, which is a 6″ spike.

BRADS are smaller and thinner than finishing nails and are used for light assembly where heads must be concealed. Sold by length rather than by penny sizes.

Craftsman's method of hiding nails is to lift a slim shaving of wood from the nail area and then drive and set the nail in the depression. The shaving is then glued back to its original position. When neatly done, no trace of the nail is visible.

RECOMMENDED NAILS FOR PLYWOOD

Plywood Thickness	Type of Nail	Size
¾″	casing	6d
	finishing	6d
⅝″	finishing	6d–8d
½″	finishing	4d–6d
⅜″	finishing	3d–4d
¼″	brads	¾″–1″
	finishing	3d
	lath	1″

WOOD FINISHING

THE CHOICE OF MATERIALS

As you know, a finish is a combination of material and a method. There are differences—some slight, some enormous—between the *way you handle* the various materials, and the way they perform for you.

Each major finishing material has particular preparation, handling, and application requirements, which are described in this section. Your choice of finish will depend on several factors: the type of wood or the use which the completed project will be subject to; the look you expect to obtain as a result of finishing; and the characteristics of the finishing materials themselves. There are important differences in varnish, shellac, and lacquer, in their own properties, how they are applied, and in preparation of the wood. You will want to note their "color" characteristics, ease or difficulty of application, drying times, and lasting qualities.

VARNISH, SHELLAC, LACQUER

Varnish is the most popular clear finish for wood because it is fairly easy to use, provides good durability, and gives a color well liked by most people. Its durable, clear coating is often selected for furniture, floors, trim, and all other forms of natural wood finishes, including brightwork on boats. It is made by mixing tough resins in oil-derived vehicles, along with dryers and other chemicals which provide such characteristics as semigloss drying when it is desired. When the vehicle evaporates, a film of resins remains, stuck tight to the wood. In most cases this film is dust-free in an hour to four hours, ready for handling in about eight hours, and dry enough for sanding and recoat in about twenty-four hours. Some special varnishes are made of resins which are hard in about eight hours, but do not reach full "cure" for perhaps a week.

The resins used in today's varnishes are usually alkyd, phenolic, or urethane. Alkyds are synthetic oils, often used in quality exterior and interior paints. Phenolics are resins with a formaldehyde base that are especially well suited for exterior use, including use as a clear finish over brass and other brightwork and as marine-grade or "spar" varnishes. Urethane or polyurethane (polymer) varnishes are made with synthetic plastic resins and are perhaps the hardest and most durable varnish finishes. Unlike other varnishes, urethanes resist crazing and chipping, and they are highly resistant to water, alcohol, chemicals and heat. Urethanes are so tough once cured, however, that they are difficult to remove. They also have a sensitive period after the first application, during which time a second coat must be applied or proper adhesion of further coats cannot be assured.

The color varnish gives to wood is basically the result of oils it contains. It intensifies wood tones, tending to darken dark areas proportionately more than light areas, thus increasing the pattern of wood grain. The general effect is to give the wood warmth—a reddishness. You can get a quick close approximation of the color by brushing turpentine or linseed oil on a sample of the wood.

Some varnishes have a slight yellow color, the natural hue of the resins. There may be a tendency for this yellow hue to deepen as the finish ages. Older varnishes turned almost orange with time; new resins, particularly the urethanes, are lighter and go yellow very slightly.

"Synthetic" varnishes, some of them containing acrylic and vinyl resins, are extremely clear and do not change color at all. Their only shortcoming is a tenderness as far as abrasion is concerned.

By far the most interesting (and recent) of these is *water-thinned* varnish, a product that is part of the finishing-chemistry industry's trend toward materials that are easier and safer to use. In oversimplified terms, the industry has added chemicals to the formulas that make those tough resins soluble in—mixable with—water, instead of in petroleum-derived thinners. Once they have dried, however, they are just as tough as their petroleum-thinned cousins.

The major advantage is the way brushes wash clean with soap and water—sometimes even more quickly and easily than we have come to expect with latex paints. Another feature you'll discover in some of the water-thinned clear finishes—varnishes—is the way they go on.

The flow-out is good. The application has a milky appearance as it goes on, and you can judge the uniformity of coverage by the degree of milkiness. As it dries, it turns clear.

The durability of varnish is excellent—unsurpassed in some respects. Urethane and polyurethane varnishes have the highest resistance to abrasion and to ordinary chemicals. Those based on other resins, such as alkyds and phenolics, have slightly less

Basic Characteristics of Varnishes

Kind of varnish	Sheen	Color effect	Protection	Number of coats	Drying time	How to apply
Glossy	High shine	Darkens wood. Pale to quite yellow film.	Excellent	2 or 3	24 hours	Brush or spray
Semi-gloss	Low shine	Same	Good	1 or 2. If more are needed, start with gloss.	24 hours	Brush or spray
Satin	Lustre	Same	Good	Same	24 hours	Brush or spray
Flat	Low lustre	Same	Fair	Same	24 hours	Brush or spray
Urethane	Available in gloss, semi-gloss satin, and flat	Darkens wood. Film is quite pale.	Superior in gloss. Excellent in dulls.	Same	Varies. See labels.	Brush or spray
Vinyl	Gloss or semi	Darkens wood less. Film is quite pale.	Good except abrasion	Same	15 minutes. See labels.	Brush or spray
Oil	None	Darkens wood	Poor	Many. See text.	See text.	Brush or swab

resistance to abrasion and to chemicals. They tend, however, to be brittle. For this reason they scratch "white," and may show a fine network of cracks in time, particularly if the wood is subjected to wide changes in humidity. The wood swells and shrinks in a degree greater than the varnish film can handle. In extreme cases the varnish actually chips off.

The drying time is fast, making it possible to put on two or three coats in a single day, as opposed to the coat-a-day schedule most often approved for regular varnish.

Give the water-thinned material a try. You may be willing to overlook their tendency to raise the grain in view of the fact that they give wood all the beauty you get from oil-based finishes.

Varnish is among the more difficult materials to apply well, although it goes on slapdash with great ease when the work is uncritical. A good varnish brushes easily and levels well. It will hold a good coat on vertical surfaces without sagging. But due to slow drying, it is extremely difficult to avoid dust marks, unless you can work in an area that is entirely dust-free. There are techniques for overcoming dust marks—but they represent some extra work.

You can buy good varnish in spray cans—and you can use it in regular spray guns. Results are excellent in both cases—subject however to the same problems with dust.

PREPARING THE SURFACE FOR VARNISH

Since the wood shows through varnish—the more it shows the better—it must be as nearly perfect as possible before you put on the first coat.

Bare wood. Examine the project thoroughly for dirt, finger marks, streaks caused by abrasion, and other blemishes. Clean them off with mineral spirits, lacquer thinner, or a multisolvent product. If necessary, sand, but if you sand, use the finest paper and run over the entire area which is blemished. Otherwise, the freshly sanded area may not take the coloration from the varnish evenly.

Stained wood. Be sure stains have had adequate drying time. Give the stain job a last minute inspection, to see if there are any places where they are too dark and might produce muddy areas. Lighten these areas carefully, using fine steel wool on pigmented wiping stains and the proper solvent on water stains or non-grain-raising stains—i.e., water or NGR thinner. Do not forget that varnish will change the color of the stained wood. As the chapter on stains explained, you should make tests in advance of stain-plus-varnish to determine the exact shade. If

you have not already done this, you may want to put a brush-stroke of varnish in an inconspicuous spot as a last minute check. If the color is not right, you can darken it slightly with a reapplication of diluted stain or lighten it as mentioned above. If you add more stain, be sure to wait the proper drying time.

Old finishes. When an old finish is in good enough shape so that it needs nothing more than a rejuvenating coat of new varnish, make sure that it is absolutely clean. Wash it with detergent and water and rinse, or mop it with mineral spirits, lacquer thinner, or a product such as Liquid Sandpaper or Wilbond. All oil, wax, grease, and other contamination must be removed. If the surface is glossy, scarify it with fine sandpaper, to insure good adhesion.

DUST IS THE ENEMY OF VARNISH

No matter how carefully you work—unless it is in an air-filtered, humidity-controlled, sanitary room—you'll have trouble with dust. What you must do is eliminate as much of it as possible, then learn what to do about that which, inevitably, remains.

To begin with, dust is the biggest headache when you use a glossy varnish and leave the final coat glossy—that is, unrubbed. Dust *on* the surface or which *settles on* the freshly applied varnish forms tiny pinnacles as the varnish accumulates around the dust speck. If there are only a few such specks, you can take care of them with a picking stick or a small artist's brush. If there are many, the finish that is intended to be slick and smooth turns out to be toothy and rough.

A little dust is less of a problem with rubbed finishes, since the rubbing eliminates the tiny pinnacles. This is one reason why many finishers consider a rubbed finish easier to do than a truly fine glossy finish.

APPLICATION TECHNIQUES FOR VARNISH

The first coat of varnish on bare wood or wood colored with water or NGR stains should be thinned with about 1 part of turpentine to 4 parts of varnish. Brush this coat out well, using it as a sealer. *When you seal with the same varnish as you'll use for the rest of the job, you get better results. You do not run the risk of different characteristics fighting each other on the wood.* For instance, if you seal with a material which has a different degree of flexibility, you set up stresses between the sealer and the varnish, which will eventually cause the finish to fail. Many of the best varnish practitioners, working for a perfect job, even use thinned varnish as a sanding base for the final smoothing.

Always try to varnish with a white wall or a window in back of the work, so that you can watch the glare – the shiny area in this photo. It will tell you quickly if you are over-applying. If you are skipping – and if you are picking up dust. The tiny dark specks on the varnished area shown here are dust specks which you could pick up with a picking stick – see text.

Over a pigmented wiping stain, which already contains resins which seal, you can use varnish without thinning.

Second and all subsequent coats should be used as they come from the can unless you find that there is too much drag on the brush. If this is the case, use a very small amount of turpentine. Stir slowly—to avoid bubbles—but thoroughly. If possible, let the varnish with turpentine stirred in stand for a few hours, to homogenize.

These coats of varnish should be full, but not puddled. With a little experimentation and practice you will learn to put on the exact amount of varnish *which will level.* If you use too little, you'll see skimpy spots where there is too little varnish to flow out smoothly. If you use too much—more than is needed for leveling—drying time will be overlong. And, you run the risk of crazing and checking later on.

How to brush varnish smoothly. Whenever possible, work on horizontal surfaces. Disassemble a piece if you can—removing drawers, doors, etc., so they can be laid flat. Tack up a piece of white paper or a white sheet, or work in front of a white wall, so that you can easily observe the glare produced by well-leveled varnish.

Give the surface one last swipe with the tack rag, then start at the far edge and work toward you. Work out any method of laying the varnish on that is easiest. Most professionals lay on two or three brush-wide stripes with about a brush-width between them. Then they brush crosswise to smooth out. Finally they tip off the varnish using just the ends of the bristles. Brush handling is illustrated in the accompanying photographs. The standard advice is to dip only one-third of the bristles into the varnish. Violate this rule if you want to; dip less, dip more, depending on whether you are going fast over a large surface or working slowly over a small area or around carvings. When you first dip the brush, massage it for a few seconds against the side of the can, to work the varnish well into the bristles.

Continue laying on varnish, smoothing, then tipping until the entire surface is covered. Generally, it is best to work from end to end of an area that is longer than it is wide rather than from edge to edge. As you complete each cycle of lay-on, smooth-out, tip-off, make a final leveling tipping stroke from the new varnish into the varnish just applied. Observe this operation carefully, and watch for any lack of smoothness. If the joining strip doesn't level out in a minute or two, it is a sign that you should go through the three-stage cycle over a smaller area, since the edge is beginning to set a little before you get back to it. With practice you'll learn just how large an area you can cover and still show no lapmarks.

Do not slap-slap varnish on. Stroke smoothly and slowly, or you may whip up bubbles. Sometimes bubbles break quickly and the varnish levels. Too often, however, bubbles break after the varnish starts to set, and the result is a small depression which is difficult to sand out.

Use the tack rag, wiping the unvarnished surface as you go along. It will save lots of work later on.

Special problems of curved surfaces.
Carvings, moldings, and other surfaces which are not flat present problems in that the irregularities tend to squeegee varnish off the brush in greater quantities than necessary, causing sags and puddling. For that reason, work with a fairly dry brush on irregular surfaces.

Rounds and turnings. The best method of handling round legs, spindles, stretchers, and the like is to apply the varnish by brushing back and forth across the round. Then, level with lengthwise strokes. Usually, when spindles are small, you work better with a smaller brush than you'd use on flat surfaces.

Moldings. Regular moldings, such as ogee, cove and bead, etc., which are not carved (as are egg-and-dart and others) are simple to handle with lengthwise strokes. If you brush across moldings, you usually fill the depressions and skimp the high ridges.

Carvings. Putting varnish on intricate carvings is more lifting than brushing. First, spread the varnish over the carved area. Dab

it well into crevices and deep depressions. Then, by placing the brush in carvings and lifting it out with a gentle brushing motion, you gradually dry up the over-wet areas. Strike the excess off your brush by pulling it across the lip of your varnish can. If dust has accumulated in the carvings, the varnish you pull out will be filled with it. Dispose of this dusty varnish by striking it off on the edge of a tin can, which you can then throw away. (Use such worthless varnish to make tack rags, picking sticks.)

True panels. The proper method of applying finish to a true panel—for instance, a paneled door—is to do the panel first, then the frame. As you coat the broad surface, catch the inner edge of the frame. Then pull out the excess varnish gathered in the crack, by putting the tips of the bristles in the crack and brushing gently away. Finally do the frame and the edges.

Corners and edges. If you let a brush stroke go over an edge or an outside corner, you will leave sags on vertical surfaces and what finishers call a ''fat edge'' on horizontal surfaces. To avoid this, all smoothing and tipping strokes *must start on the flat* and go toward the edge. *Precisely at the edge,* lift the brush so that the bristles take off before they can flip over the edge and leave an extra-thick deposit of varnish. If you start the tipping strokes in the air, gently lowering the brush while it is in motion, you won't leave starting marks on the flat. Master this lift-off at the edges and you'll never be guilty of leaving a sag or a fat edge.

Inside corners—such as the point where shelves meet uprights—should be pulled out, to prevent a thick fillet of varnish.

How to use a picking stick. A picking stick is a splinter of wood with a small glob of sticky rosin on the end. It looks something like a wooden match; the rosin is the head. To make one, first dissolve a small amount of powdered rosin in varnish. (Buy a rosin bag at a sporting goods store or a chunk of violin bow rosin at a music store and crush it.) The mixture should be about as thick as cold honey. Dip the tip of the stick in it, moisten your fingers, and roll the glob of rosin into a ball. Dip it again, and roll again. This is a picking stick. Its gummy end will pick up a speck of dust.

Sighting at a low angle, so that dust specks are easy to see, touch the stick carefully to each tiny dust-caused pinnacle. Roll the dust speck into the glob with moistened fingers. Be careful not to press the stick into the finish, or you may make a crater which will not level again. Normally, however, the tiny depression made when you lift out the varnish speck will fill and level.

You can do a minor amount of dust picking with a small artist's brush or even with the split end of a wooden splinter or a broken toothpick, but a regular picking stick is worth the bother of making; it works much better.

Loose bristles. When a bristle loosens from the brush and lies in the varnish, pick it up by jabbing at one end of it gently with the tips of the bristles. It will lodge between bristles and you can pick it off with your

Proper brush angle for varnish—or any other finish—is about 45 degrees, so that the ''chisel'' of the brush meets the surface and puts the maximum amount of bristle in contact with the wood. The proper degree of bend in the bristles is shown here, too.

Avoid what you see in this photo – the brush falling over the edge of a surface. It produces a ''fat edge'' because the edge squeegees extra varnish off the brush. Drying is slow, rubbing is difficult, and the result is as much of a woodfinishing disgrace as is a sag.

fingers. A quick brush stroke levels the varnish where you picked up the bristle.

SHELLAC

Wood finishers often use shellac almost any place you'd use varnish, although it is not as water-resistant. Some of the most beautiful finishes are done with shellac. The vehicle in shellac is denatured alcohol, and the resin is a natural gum secreted by an insect called the lac bug, found in India and neighboring countries. The gum, cleaned and refined, is dissolved in alcohol. In use, you dilute shellac even further with alcohol, producing a thin liquid which brushes easily, flows out smooth, dries quickly.

Shellac comes in two colors: white and orange. The latter has a deep amber cast. On the wood, however, there is very little difference, and most finishers use the white in all cases. On the other hand, there are experts who prefer the orange on dark woods, the white on light-colored species.

Shellac gives wood a warmth and fire similar to that produced by varnish. Only personal experimentation will tell you which you like best. On woods such as cherry, mahogany, walnut, teak, rosewood, and other dark species, the color is particularly good.

No great claims for durability can be made for shellac in situations of hard usage. It is smooth enough and flexible enough to withstand normal wear, and it does not scratch white the way a brittle varnish does. It resists the tendency to check, craze, and flake off. On projects which are not likely to suffer

Excellent but rarely used technique with relatively thin-bodied brushing lacquers is dipping, as shown here with an ebony and ivory cufflink. A good trick is to suspend such small objects on a wire with an L-bent end, then whirl it so that centrifugal force takes off the excess, after a quick drain into the can.

abuse from water, chemicals, strong detergents, and particularly alcohol, you can expect a lot of life from shellac. Even on floors, it gives excellent performance, particularly when it is reinforced with a good wax job. But—if a primary consideration is toughness there are better materials.

One of the major reasons for the popularity of shellac is the easy way it goes on. Thinned with alcohol to a consistency not much thicker than water, it flows out and leaves brush strokes with virtually no edges. Quick to dry, it lets you knock off the high spots with 6/0 or finer sandpaper and recoat in an hour or so. Thus, the multicoat requirement of shellac is often offset entirely by the ease and speed with which each coat goes on.

Shellac, like varnish, comes in spray cans. Although this form presents some convenience, it takes away your ability to thin shellac to your liking for good built-up finishes. And, with the spray can, you lost the economic advantage of shellac's low cost.

LACQUER

The third of the major clear finishes, lacquer involves still another type of resin—usually cellulose nitrate in combination with man-made materials. However, some of the newer resins are used in modern lacquers, including acrylic, vinyl, and others. Owing to a rather loose lexicography in the paints and finishing industry, lacquer and varnish seem to overlap somewhat, and an acrylic clear may be thought of as a varnish by one manufacturer and as a lacquer by another. This is further complicated by the growing use of petroleum derivatives in finishing materials which formerly contained acetates. Modern lacquers have vehicles which are highly sophisticated blends of acetates, alcohols, and hydrocarbons, and through the control of resins and vehicle components, lacquers can be made slow-drying (to be brushed on) or fast-drying (for spraying only). When you shop, keep in mind that you can put on a brushing lacquer by brush *or* spray, but you cannot handle a spraying lacquer with a brush. It sets up too quickly.

Lacquers are usually water-clear, and their effect on the color of the wood is much like that of water. They intensify grain and color, but do not materially change the hue. There is a special variety of brushing lacquer called "lightener" which leaves the color of the wood virtually unchanged. Use it whenever you want the final finish to retain the color of the original wood.

The ability of lacquer to withstand abuse is good, as indicated by its wide use on floors. The lacquer film is hard, difficult to scratch. But it has low flexibility and usually shows a tendency to craze after a year or two. Most

furniture factories spray on a lacquer finish, the fastest method for mass production.

Brushing lacquers, used thin and in multiple coats, are easy to use, comparable to shellac. They rub well, and you can build any thickness of film with good adhesion between coats.

TIPS ON USING LACQUER

Since most people have had much more experience with varnish than with lacquer, the best way to spell out the tricks of lacquer application is to contrast them with varnish.

1. Instead of laying the material on, then smoothing it, you should attempt to flow lacquer on in a good wet coat without too much brushback. Move fast, using long strokes. Keep a wet edge by working in small areas. Usually a relatively long and narrow area is easiest to handle. To keep the action fast, use a wider brush that you might like for varnish. Never apply lacquer with a tiny brush unless the project itself is tiny. Width rather than fullness is the mark of a good lacquer brush, which needn't have bristles as long as are considered best for varnish.

2. Instead of using lacquer as thick as you can brush it comfortably, as you do with varnish, keep it thin enough to flow out well. This may mean some thinner, even in a material such as Satinlac, which is canned at a brushable consistency as it is. Be sure to buy a good thinner. There are many chemicals which will reduce the consistency of lacquer, but not all of them produce good results. Thin all coats, if necessary.

3. Sanding between coats is not necessary with lacquer *to provide adhesion.* Each coat tends to soften the preceding one minutely, bonding to it. Thus, scarifying for mechanical bond, as with varnish, doesn't help. However, you may want to scuff-sand enough to knock off high spots and the few dust specks you'll be bound to get, even with lacquer. And, if you are working toward a high rubbed finish, similar to the so-called piano finish, you will always *sand to plane* the surface, if application is rough. Do not use water on between-coat sanding with lacquer. Be sure to give lacquer at least four hours to dry before sanding and recoating. Dry the final coat overnight, before you do the last stages of rubbing with pumice.

When using lacquer, you may encounter any one of several difficulties. But these can be handled if you know how.

Orange peel. You may get this when you spray if your pressure is not high enough for the viscosity of the lacquer. Instructions that come with spray guns cover the use of viscosity meters and other methods of making sure that lacquer is the right thickness for spraying. Another cause of the pebbled look of orange peel is spraying from too far away, allowing the minute particles of lacquer to harden slightly while they are in the air. You may get this result with spray cans as well as with standard compressor sprayers. Move in slightly, and be sure that you are spraying wet. Bad thinners cause orange peel, too.

Pinholes. Several spraying mistakes cause tiny holes in the surface, caused by vapor-pressure of solvents beneath a surface film which forms quickly. In other words, too much surface drying for the character of the coat. With big spraying equipment, the reason is most often improper thinners. With spray cans, the problem usually comes from spraying too wet. With either type of spraying, you get pinholes by spraying the second coat too soon. The previous coat is still emitting vapors first, bubbles, then pinholes when the bubbles burst.

Sags. Spraying too heavily causes sags and runs, just as brushing too heavily does. However, spraying with too little drying time can be worse. May you be spared the vision of an entire finish softening and sliding off the wood because you sprayed too many coats too soon—and they all softened and sagged at once.

Bleeding. Rosewood, particularly, but also mahogany and some other woods contain pigments which are soluble in the solvents of lacquer. Also, some stains are softened and brought into solution by these solvents. To complicate things further, certain fillers and sealers are softened by lacquer. These are the reasons why you should always use a ''lacquer compatible'' system throughout. Commercial finishing involves lacquer-base fillers and sealers. You cannot buy these materials at typical paint stores, however. So, the best practices involving easily procurable materials are as follows:

1. Use water or NGR stains. If you find it necessary to use a pigmented wiping stain, give it at least forty-eight hours to dry. Otherwise, the lacquer thinners may act like paint and varnish removers.

2. Give any standard paste filler forty-eight hours to set up hard, for the same reason.

3. A safeguard is the use of thinned shellac as a sealer after stains or filler or both.

4. Use a lacquer-type sander-sealer-filler unless the wood is of such open grain that paste fillers are required.

5. Let everything dry thoroughly, in advance of lacquering, especially any oil-resin or petroleum derivative materials.

6. When you plan to use lacquer over rosewood or dark mahogany, use a thin shellac washcoat as a sealer and *do not sand it.* The shellac will seal the pigment, keeping it from bleeding, and you might cut through it if you sand, thus breaking the seal.

PENETRATING FINISHES

Finally, your choice may be a penetrating finish—one that is entirely in the wood, never on it. The in-the-wood finishes grow in popularity every day, not only because they are so easy to use, but because they give wood a fantastic amount of protection without obscuring its beauty in any way. Penetrating finishes are little used on trim, but are excellent on floors, on furniture, paneling, cabinets, and other interior jobs.

DANISH OILS

Also called penetrating resins or antique oil finishes, these are usually linseed or tung oil based with petroleum distillates and synthetic or natural resins added. The distillates help the oil penetrate the wood and then, being volatile, aid in drying as they quickly evaporate, leaving behind the resins which provide a durable finish. Oils of this type are sometimes heat-processed or polymer-ized to create a tougher-curing finish. Examples include Watco's Danish Oil Finish, McCloskey's Tungseal and Antique Oil Finish from Minwax. Finishing oils are usually rubbed into the wood's surface by hand until they are thoroughly absorbed, imparting a lustrous yet invisible sheen to the wood; repeated applications, with light rubbing by fine steel wool between coats, builds a glossier finish that is impervious to water, alcohols and most other solvents. Oil finishes can be renewed at any time by simply buffing lightly and adding a thin coat of oil with a lintless cloth pad or with your bare hand.

LINSEED OIL

Once considered one of the best natural finishes, this oil made from the flax (linen) seed has lost favor in recent years to the many new or reformulated penetrating finishes now available to home woodworkers. Linseed oil's decline in popularity is due to several reasons, however. It doesn't dry as quickly or as thoroughly as other natural and synthetic finishes; it turns dark and, on some woods, black with age; and it attracts mildew when used on wood subjected to dampness. A fine hand-rubbed finish may be achieved by using boiled linseed oil mixed with equal parts of turpentine and furniture-grade varnish.

TUNG OIL

Perhaps the most versatile natural finishing oil and one favored by woodworkers for its superior drying and sealing qualities. It is sold and used either raw (100% pure), polymerized in varying degrees for different wood finishing applications, or formulated with other oils and additives. Pure tung oil is available from the Hope Company, and a variety of polymerized tung oils are produced by Sutherland Welles Ltd.

FURNITURE WAXES

With the increased use of synthetic sealers and impermeable, all-purpose wood finishes of consistent quality, waxing furniture is in many cases unnecessary and often simply a matter of choice. Varnished woodwork doesn't need additional protection, but occasional waxing will help maintain and increase the finish's lustre. Oil finished wood, on the other hand, often has a desired low-lustre sheen that a waxy shine will only obscure. Waxing should only be done on very smooth, close-grained woods or open-grained woods that have been finished with a sanding sealer or wood filler. No amount of waxing will produce a high shine on wood that has not been properly finish-sanded, and wax used on unfilled, open-grained wood such as oak will clog the wood's pores, spoiling rather than enhancing the finish. Waxes also build up on the wood surface after repeated applications, attracting dirt and requiring periodic stripping with solvents such as mineral spirits or turpentine. The major furniture waxes are carnauba (palm) wax, natural beeswax, and petroleum-based paraffin. Carnauba is the hardest drying wax but it is difficult to buff to a high gloss; it is frequently mixed with beeswax or paraffin, both of which are too soft to be used alone. Well-known brands include Butcher's Bowling Al-

ley Wax (clear and amber), and Paste Finishing Wax (all-purpose and Special Type for dark or unfilled wood surfaces) by Minwax.

SOME WOODS DEMAND CERTAIN FINISHES

One of the most important considerations in selecting a finish is the wood itself. Some species—mahogany, for instance—can be finished almost any way—stained, bleached, filled, natural, in-the-wood. Others don't seem right unless they have one specific finish. A good example is teak, which in the eyes of most finishers would be profaned by anything other than a penetrating, in-the-wood finish which reveals the texture and the grain. The rule of thumb is that fine-grain woods are best with finishes that build on the surface. Maple, birch, pine, cherry, gum, basswood, beech, and similar species may be sealed with a penetrating finish, for good adhesion, but their topcoats should be varnish, shellac, or lacquer rubbed, glossy, or semiglossy.

Open-pore woods such as oak, mahogany, chestnut, pecan, walnut, ash, and the like look right with a penetrating finish or one that is on the surface. Here the choice depends on the nature of the project. Traditional mahogany was nearly always done with a filled, smooth, rubbed finish; for that reason, traditionally styled pieces you finish or refinish should be smooth. With modern mahogany, open-pore finishes may be more appropriate. This is true with walnut too. However, the absolute opposite approach is used with oak. Traditional oak was always open-pore finished and much of it had no finish at all. Oak used in modern design is filled more often than not—sometimes with a colored filler which makes a novelty of the wood pores.

ENAMEL FINISHES

Most of us think of enamel as the colored material paint dealers carry in dozens of colors, in cans from half-pints or smaller up to gallons. That is the most common, and perhaps the most useful kind. A good quality enamel of this sort is actually nothing more than a good varnish with pigments added in sufficient quantity to give the finish opacity and color. And, like varnishes, enamels are now being produced in water-thinnable formulas. This makes possible all the qualities of oil-based enamels with the advantages of latex-type enamels.

The good alkyd enamels, as this might suggest, are handled exactly like varnish, when you're shooting for a good colored finish.

In the paint industry, however, the general category called "enamel" also includes colored lacquers. Again—the material is nothing more than a lacquer formulated with pigments to give it color and hiding power. For most home-workshop finishers, colored lacquer means spray cans of lacquer, such as Krylon, DuPont Spray Paint, and others. Now and then, you'll find a few cans of colored lacquer on a dealer's shelves; it is nearly always spraying lacquer, as is most colored lacquer.

There is, however, an excellent source for high-quality color lacquers, if you have spraying equipment and want to use them: your auto supply dealer. You can buy lacquer the color of any automobile manufactured in the past ten years or so—just to give you an idea of the color range possible. (As a matter of fact, you can match those colors in oil-resin automobile enamel, which is usually of quality unmatched in ordinary enamels.) As with oleo-resin enamels, a good colored lacquer is handled exactly like clear lacquer.

Colored brushing lacquer is difficult to find. You can thin spraying lacquers with materials which are slow-drying—relatively—and retard drying time enough so that brushing is possible. Such thinners include amyl acetate, butyl acetate, and others. However, a colored lacquer thinned enough for each brushing usually *carries so little color* that you need coat after coat after coat to build both surface and color. For that reason, you should consider lacquer in colors as a spray-only material. Use the spray cans, which give excellent results, or use a regular spray gun.

Enamels come in glossy and semiglossy—and in a variety called "flat enamel" which fits better in the category of paint and which is intended more for painting walls than for finishing wood. The difference between glossy and semiglossy in enamels is basically the same as in varnishes. Pigments break up the surface of the semiglosses so that they have a velvet look.

There are further differences, however. The glossies are normally put up in a *deeper range of colors,* going into dark blues, greens, browns, reds. They are also put up in pastels. The semigloss enamels, on the other hand, are rarely packaged in dark shades. The reason for this is that satinsheen enamels are generally intended to be used as trim colors to match wall paint; there is no real reason why semigloss enamel can't be factory-packaged in the same colors as glossy, other than normal demand. You can, however, obtain semiglossy enamel any color you want in the *custom-color systems* which nearly every paint store has. In very dark shades, semigloss enamels run up in cost, due to the amount of pigment it takes to make them. At the same time, the relatively high proportion of pigments to vehicle makes dark-colored semiglossies less durable—less resistant to abrasion, water, and other damage. Many times, a dark-hued semigloss

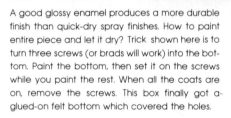

A good glossy enamel produces a more durable finish than quick-dry spray finishes. How to paint entire piece and let it dry? Trick shown here is to turn three screws (or brads will work) into the bottom. Paint the bottom, then set it on the screws while you paint the rest. When all the coats are on, remove the screws. This box finally got a glued-on felt bottom which covered the holes.

is slow to dry, and may take a week or more to harden thoroughly.

For these reasons, semigloss enamel in dark colors should be your choice only for projects too large to rub, or for parts of a project which are not worth rubbing. To cite an example, you might use a semigloss enamel on the sides and drawer fronts of a chest, but go to the bother of a rubbed enamel finish on the top.

HOW TO DO A RUBBED ENAMEL FINISH

Using a good glossy enamel or a good spraying lacquer or a spray can of lacquer, you

Handle enamel as you do varnish or lacquer, building up a flat finish with wet-sandpaper rubbing between coats.

can build up a finish that in color is the exact counterpart of a rubbed finish in clear varnish or lacquer.

When you are shooting for a top-grade finish with enamel, your brushwork must be as careful as it is with varnish. Using the same tactics, follow these steps:

First, lay on the enamel in stripes the width of your brush over an area that is comfortable to work with. Have these stripes heavy—twice as thick as you want the final coating—and have them spaced about a brush width apart.

Second, brush out these stripes, crosswise, smoothing the enamel over the entire area.

Third, tip off the enamel with gentle, even strokes lengthwise, letting only the tips of the bristles touch. Hold the brush quite vertical for tipping off, and you'll produce fewer bubbles. When one section is finished, move to the next, and blend them together as you brush out and tip off.

There is a reversal of procedures which you might want to use, however.

You may want to build a short-cut non-gloss finish by putting on two or three coats of *glossy* varnish, then topcoat this build with a semigloss material. The result is a fairly good substitute for a rubbed finish. A short-cut method of building a rubbed enamel is to build levels with the extra-bodied semigloss. Rub between coats, until the surface is absolutely plane and smooth. Then put on a coat of glossy enamel for the top coat. Since you do not have to carry the color with this coat, and since the surface beneath it is already quite plane, you can hit the glossy coat with a sanding block and 6/0 paper, then switch to pumice and oil to complete the rubbing. Few finishes of any kind are more beautiful than a well-rubbed build of enamel which is finally coated with a good buffing of paste wax.

Another difference between enamels and varnishes or lacquers is that you do not normally use fillers under them. Partly this is because the pigments in the enamel tend to fill, but of equal importance is the fact that you do not often put colored finishes over the walnuts, mahoganies, teaks, and other woods which are so porous as to require filling for a good, level clear finish. This does not excuse you from a thorough sanding and cleaning of the surface.

ENAMEL UNDERCOATERS

Most enamels specify the use of an enamel undercoater as the first coat. The undercoater has several advantages. It is cheaper than enamel and therefore gives you a first coat at less cost. Its special formulation provides an ideal surface for enameling, and in many cases makes it possible to complete a colored finish in two coats, since you can put more enamel on over an undercoater without the danger of sags and runs.

However, for small jobs, the undercoater is more nuisance than its advantages warrant, and actually represents a cost increase; it's a can you might not have needed. Moreover, it is usually white. This is all right if you are enameling white. But when your enamel is in a color, you must tint the undercoater or you'll never carry a very deep color enamel in one coat. Tinting is usually not feasible deeper than about medium tone. Some workers give the undercoater a little start in the right direction by pouring some of the enamel in it.

As you can see, there are many problems created by undercoaters. On the other hand, enamel itself has tremendous adhesion to a clean surface. If you thin a bit of it and use it as a primer—just as you thin varnish for the first coat—you get perfect results. Save the enamel undercoater for jobs as big as a new houseful of trim and woodwork.

HOW TO USE WOOD STAINS

KINDS OF STAINS

Ninety percent of your staining needs can be taken care of by three materials: penetrating wiping stains, water stains, and non-grain-raising (NGR) stains. These and others are covered individually below.

Pigmented wiping stains. The prototype material in this classification is Minwax. Essentially identical stains are made by virtually every paint manufacturer, with names like "oil stain," "wood finish," "wood stain," etc. These stains are a penetrating oil-resin vehicle in which *pigments* have been stirred. The pigments are not in solution, but in suspension, and the material must be stirred rather constantly to maintain a uniform color. There may also be some color in the form of *dyes* dissolved in the liquid, but the major job of coloration is done by the solid pigments.

This family of stains includes some in a water emulsion (Deft is an example) and another that comes in a tube—toothpaste thick—and is one of the easiest of all stains to use (Even-Even).

The wiping stains tend to leave the most pigment in pores, in softwood areas, in blemishes. This means that they greatly accentuate the grain pattern, as well as any places which are not properly and smoothly sanded. Woods that are soft and porous, such as pecan, lauan, fir, etc., accept a great deal of stain, darkening greatly. Harder woods such as maple, birch, beech, etc., take less stain. Walnut, mahogany, oak, and similar hardwoods with open pores accumulate a lot of the pigment in their pores.

Although pigmented wiping stains come in all the regular woodtone colors (plus more) and are regularly used on any and all woods, they perform their best magic on pine and

Although a cardinal rule for finishing is to stain over clean wood only, now and then you slip. When some sort of dirt holds a stain out, try rubbing it in with a small piece of steel wool. The slight abrasion helps the stain penetrate.

other softwoods. Owing to the way cracks, dents, and scratches catch the pigment, wiping stains are excellent for any "distressed" finish, as well as for furniture and paneling in the "primitive" style.

Application of pigmented wiping stains—covered in detail later on—is very simple.

Water stains. These are true stains, in that they *dye the fibers of the wood* the way cloth is dyed. The colors are brilliant, stable even in sunlight. Penetration tends to be uniform, even in woods that have widely varying porosity, such as fir plywood.

Water stains are very inexpensive. For something like 30 cents each you buy packets of dye powders. These usually have wood-hue names and are blends of aniline dyes produced by a chemical dye house. Also, there are pure colors—black, red, green, etc. You dissolve a packet of dye powder in a quart of water close to boiling. This forms a stock solution which you may use straight—dilute with water for lighter shades—or modify with other water stains. Not all paint and hardware stores stock these dry powders, but they can order them for you.

There is much variation in stain colors from one line to another. A packet labeled "walnut" may be three different colors from three different manufacturers. For this reason you may have to experiment a little to find the colors that please you best. Some dye powders are labeled "water & alcohol soluble," and as the name suggests will dissolve in either water or alcohol or both. These powders do not produce the same color in alcohol (which produces cold, somewhat greenish tones) as in water (which produces warm, reddish tones). One of the most interesting and subtle blendings of stain colors comes from varying proportions of water and alcohol with aniline powders which dissolve in either or both.

Non-grain-raising stains. Stains which do not use water—or use only a relatively small amount of water—do not cause the grain to raise, since the liquids they employ do not soften the fibers. NGR stains (sometimes called NFR, for "non-fiber-raising") based on chemical by-products of the petroleum industry have about the same qualities as water stains, but dry for topcoating in a few hours. The colors are a bit more intense than those of water stains when they dry—but they are close to identical in brilliance under topcoatings. The NGR stains are considered, largely, to be industrial products and for that reason they are hard to buy at retail. They come in quart bottles (or bigger) and it is a good idea to order thinner at the same time; you'll rarely use an NGR straight. These stains can be thinned with wood alcohol, if necessary, however.

You can make your own NGR stains, if you wish, using alcohol soluble powders and wood (denatured) alcohol. This stain will dry a bit faster than commercially prepared NGR, but you can slow it down by adding a *small* quantity of water. Although this would seem to destroy the non-grain-raising properties, the small amount of water does not raise the grain enough to become a factor in the finishing.

NGR stains are not recommended for pine, fir, spruce, and similar woods with wide variation in density between spring and summer growth, since the grain pattern may go wild. They are, however, high favorites on the standard cabinet woods and are pretty much the universal stain used in furniture factories.

Oil stains. Although some pigmented wiping stains are labeled "oil stain," they are not true stains in that they contain solid pigments. True oil stains are composed of an oil-base vehicle in which oil-soluble dyes are dissolved. They penetrate the wood and permeate the fibers with color. These materials are not very common, appearing nowadays mainly in products which closely resemble *colored* penetrating resin sealers.

Varnish stains. Some surfaces never invite a close look—such as insides of cabinets, backs of chests, bed rails, and the like. These may not merit the bother of the same finish

Pigmented wiping stains are ABC simple. Brush them on, let them penetrate for a few minutes, then wipe off. Penetration time controls darkness of stain. Be sure to wipe clean – or the pigment tends to obscure the wood.

The final color of a finish comes from the stain plus the topcoating. Here a varnish is being brushed over test swatches of water stain on walnut. Each shade is a weaker dilution with water from straight to one-to-one, two-to-one, four-to-one, etc. If your project involves turnings, make tests on a prototype turning.

you'd put on conspicuous spots. A coat of varnish stain in a closely matching color is a worksaver. You brush on varnish stain just as you would regular varnish. Since there are oil-soluble dyes in the material, it leaves a film on the wood which imparts a color while it obscures the wood grain to a great extent. For this reason, varnish stain works when you are using an inferior wood and want it to take on the same general hue as a better species. It saves the need for stain plus varnish or other topcoat.

Padding stains. Least known among home craftsmen is a type of stain which you apply with a wad of cheese cloth or other rag. These stains are never put into liquid form. You moisten the rag with thinned shellac or a dilute lacquer known as "padding lacquer." You touch the rag to a little colored powder and rub it over the wood until the color is spread about, usually in a pattern of shading somewhat like natural variations in wood tone.

Padding stains are *intended for use over old finishes,* and one of their major uses is for touch-up. Antique dealers often use them with burnt umber to put down a surface layer of pseudo-antiquity which is convincing enough to fool a fair judge of old furniture. Another trick is to give an off-species of wood (a cucumber panel in a cherry chest, for instance) a color that more closely matches the major wood of a piece of furniture.

Since the liquids used for padding are not of great durability or resistance to moisture,

alcohol, etc., they should have a topcoating of varnish or other protective material.

Bleaches. Although they are the precise opposite of stains, in that they remove color from the wood instead of adding it, wood lighteners belong in any discussion of wood color control. There are many chemicals (oxalic acid, Clorox, hydrogen peroxide, etc.) that will bleach wood; you'll get the best results most dependably from such two-solution products as Blanchit or Albino bleach. Two-solution bleaches are foolproof. Following instructions on the label, you apply one solution which sets up the wood, chemically, for the second solution to take away the color. With one treatment, a dark wood becomes pale. With two, it becomes pure white. Follow with a clear lacquer, to prevent yellowing.

STEPS TO A GOOD STAINING JOB

Before you open a container of stain, remind yourself that you can't do any more sanding or other preparational work after the stain goes on—except for certain patching which must match the final color. For that reason, check these points:

1. Be sure the wood is smooth or be ready to accept the consequences of roughness. Stain accentuates roughness—even the minor scratches of cross-grain sanding. There are times when you don't mind—perhaps even prefer—some roughness to be picked up by the stain. But if you don't want blemishes to show, get rid of them.

2. Be sure the wood is clean. Good uniform staining is impossible on a dirty surface, since the dirt not only may show, but it may retard penetration of the stain. The best way to be sure of a clean surface is to wipe the surface carefully with lacquer thinner.

3. Be uniform. Don't sand one area with 3/0 paper and another with 6/0. The relatively rougher 3/0 area will stain darker in many cases. Don't make the mistake of expecting a surface that has gone through a jointer or planer to be ready for stain. These tools have a burnishing, polishing effect on the wood which seals off some of its ability to absorb. These surfaces must be sanded.

4. Seal end-grain which is sure to overabsorb. Woods such as fir plywood should be sealed so that their soft and hard areas will accept stain more uniformly. On end-grain use a washcoat of shellac—about 4 parts of alcohol to 1 part of 4-pound shellac. Highly porous end-grain may take a richer mixture. Brush this washcoat on carefully, if you want uniform end-grain staining. You will find that end-grain sanded perfectly smooth with 6/0 or finer paper does not overstain, particularly with water and NGR stains. The technique of sealing soft-and-hard areas is covered in the discussion of fir plywood.

HOW TO APPLY STAIN PROPERLY

Before you stain any wood, you must establish the color you want. Most of the time, this will be a standard woodhue stain, mixed by the manufacturer. If you need to change a standard color, try experimenting with techniques covered in the following paragraphs:

To make a stain darker, add black—making sure that it is a compatible color medium. Black water stain, black NGR stain, and black (ebony) pigmented wiping stains are available. Use them to darken a stain. In the case of pigmented stains, use black pigment you buy in tubes.

To make a stain lighter, you have a choice of four methods. First, you can dilute the stain. Second, you can wipe it quickly, before penetration is great. Third, you can washcoat the wood with thin shellac to reduce penetration. Fourth, you can pretreat the wood with the solvent used in the stain, following quickly with the pure stain. This method is a variation of dilution, since the solvent already in the wood tends to weaken the stain. It is not as easy to control as the first three methods, and therefore most finishers hesitate to use it except for projects so small that they can be handled in seconds with quantities so small that diluting them would be wasteful and difficult.

NGR and water stains do not always require wiping. For that reason, the most effective means of controlling their depth is through dilution.

Penetrating wiping stains may be diluted with a penetrating sealer or a product such as Val-Oil. This reduces the amount of pigment deposited on the wood. Then, you have a further control by wiping sooner.

The final color of a stained finish is the result of the stain *plus* the topcoat. Usually the color left by the stain alone is a little flat, and a little light. When you put shellac or varnish or a penetrating sealer over it, the color intensifies and darkens. At the same time, it turns slightly warmer—that is, more reddish. When you topcoat with lacquer, the intensification is the same but the darkening is slightly less. Meanwhile, there is little effect on the warmth of the color.

Since these factors must be taken into consideration, you must experiment with these stains if the final color is critical and without tolerances. Use a sample of the identical wood, if possible—or one that is very close. Carry each experimental swatch through to topcoating.

Actual stain application can be by any method commonly used to put a finish of any kind on wood. You might as well dip a tiny project; you might as well roll a paneled wall or a floor. Spray is commonly used for water and NGR stains. Here are the basic techniques, by stain types:

Wiping stains. Although you may wipe all stains to a degree, wiping is the *key step* in the use of pigmented wiping stains. Put it on any way at all, as long as you get complete coverage. Brushing is easiest and usually neatest. Allow the material to penetrate. It is standard to wait until it starts to dull over. However, this produces the darkest coloration; wipe sooner if your color requirements demand it. *Wipe clean.* It will be impossible to remove all the pigment from the surface of the wood, but you should try. What remains in the pores and fine, almost invisible scratches provides the color.

If, after you have wiped all you can, the color is still too dark, dampen a cloth with paint thinner and *carefully* wipe more. This same technique is used in "blending"—that is, lightening certain areas which may go darker than the rest of the wood.

Blending is more often used, however, to *darken* portions of the wood which are too light—such as sapwood. When you work with pigmented wiping stains, darken these places with a second application of stain, working carefully to blend out the edges so the patch doesn't show. You may have to dilute the stain to prevent overdarkening, and will most likely find it necessary to wipe selectively, leaving a bit more pigment here and there—or a bit less—to equalize the color and produce a natural look. (Blending is done first when you use water and NGR stains.)

Pigmented wiping stains provide a degree of protection in themselves. Their vehicle is often a penetrating sealer formula. Therefore, they may need no more than a single coat of varnish or other topcoating for a complete finish. On the other hand, if you want a fine finish, rubbed and brought to a good surface, it is best to forget that there are resins in the stain. Treat it as an oil stain. Give it twelve to twenty-four hours to dry before you proceed with the finish. It is not necessary, however, to seal it with shellac as many finishers seal oil stains, since there is no tendency for the pigmented wiping stains to bleed.

Water stains. It is unfortunate that more people do not take advantage of water stains—their economy, permanence, good colors, and flexibility. They have only one drawback—which should not deter anyone in their use: water stains tend to raise the grain of the wood. Softened by the water, tiny fibers stand on end. Minute places at which the wood may have been slightly compressed by the pressures of abrasives tend to rise again, producing slight roughness. If this roughening is severe enough, you can not sand it smooth *without sanding away some or all of the stained wood.* However, very slight roughening is smoothable, if you use 6/0 or finer paper and just whisk over the surface.

The proper defense against grain raising, however, is to dampen the wood deliberately after it is entirely smooth. Then do the once-over-lightly sanding with 6/0 before you stain. The grain will not raise again. This trick is even more effective if you predampen with warm water.

Water stains produce more uniformity and less distortion of the woodgrain pattern than any other stains, and for that reason are very easy to use. You simply flood the surface with stain. Let it dry unless it seems to puddle, in which case you merely rag off the surplus. Since the water tends to occupy the wood pores and interfibrous spaces in about the same degree as the tree's sap did, the relative coloration of lighter and darker woods is about directly proportional to the natural lightness and darkness. This gives wood an honest look.

Since there is no sealing of the wood with water stains, you can put the stain on in successive coats, if you wish. This is an excellent procedure. Dilute the stain quite a bit more than required. Apply a second coat. When it is dry, put on another. Then, if necessary apply a fourth. Each application produces the same degree of darkening. You can go as slowly as you like, with no danger of overstaining.

HOW AND WHEN TO USE WOOD FILLER

No wood is entirely smooth, no matter how carefully sanded, no matter how fine-grained by nature. When the tree was growing, its trunk contained a great deal of water. When the log was sawed and planed and dried, the water disappeared, leaving spaces. In oak, chestnut, pecan, and similar woods, the holes are big. In holly, gum, and some others the pores are so small you can hardly detect them. But—holes there are, wherever saw or plane or sandpaper cut into a wood cell.

In some cases you couldn't care less; in fact, you like it that way. When you give wood a penetrating resin finish the pores stay open, and that's what makes the wood look as natural and untouched as it does.

In other cases, you don't want the wood pores to show under any conditions. If you are refinishing a Sheraton sideboard, or any other high-style traditional mahogany, you want an absolutely glass-like surface.

An obstacle to the absolutely smooth finish is that the thin film of varnish follows the hollows of the wood pores. Even after four or five coats, you can still see the pores in woods like oak and Philippine mahogany, although they pretty well disappear in maple, birch, beech, and other finer-grained species. To prevent this, use wood filler. It fills the holes. Your finish stays up on the level.

KINDS OF WOOD FILLER

The filler most commonly used is called "paste wood filler" for the reason that you buy it in a consistency about like peanut butter, although you thin it for use. This is the kind of filler used for open-pored, coarse-grained woods. It is composed of ground silicates and other solids which fill the pores up level. The finish coats ride across the filler—perfectly smooth.

The other kind of filler is much like a sanding sealer in that it is heavy-varnish consistency. It, too, contains solids, but they are usually finer and more transparent than those used for paste filler. The place for such fillers is on the finer-grained woods such as birch and maple. Many good finishers shy away from the sanding-sealer-fillers because they may give adhesion problems.

HOW TO USE PASTE WOOD FILLER

Paste wood filler is naturally a light cream color—the color of the ground solids wet with oil. You would rarely use it this color, except for a light finish on korina, prima vera, or other naturally pale wood. However, the color is a good starting place for tinting the filler any color you want, using universal colorants or pigments in oil. As with stains, the colors you'll use most often are Van Dyke brown, burnt umber, burnt sienna, and black—with white for special effects (as when making wood lighter).

The material is too thick to use as you buy it and must be thinned with turpentine or paint thinner. Do not use oil to thin paste filler; it doesn't harden well enough or soon enough to give you the smooth surface you're after. When properly thinned, wood filler is like cream—about as heavy as a good, rich wall paint. It should brush easily, but retain enough body to work into the pores of the wood and not lose much or any volume through evaporation of the thinner.

After you have thinned the filler, add the pigment. Generally speaking, unless you want some special effect, the filler should be darker than the *stained and topcoated wood.* The finish looks best if the pores of the wood show up darker than the rest of the surface. Some people like this difference to be great, and lean toward filler that is almost black. For a starter, try for a shade or two darker.

The color should match the wood—not necessarily precisely, but at least as close as the following rough formulas will provide:

Mahogany: Burnt umber. Sometimes a little rose pink, if the color is a little red. For brown mahogany, add a little black.

Walnut: Van Dyke brown. A little umber takes some of the warmth from Van Dyke.

Oak floors—clear: Just a touch of burnt umber. Too much pigment in the grain of floors makes them look dirty.

Oak floors—stained: Use the colors recommended for walnut.

Both burnt umber and Van Dyke brown are such universal woodhue colors that you can use them to darken filler for almost any wood and for almost any finish.

Some finishers use stain to tint the filler, if they are using oil or pigmented wiping stain. This practice is all right, but it is sometimes difficult to make the filler perform properly when it contains the liquids of the stain. *Remember:* the trick with wood filler is to brush on a liquid which will gradually turn back into a firm paste, so that it will stay in the wood pores.

Brushing the filler on. You scrub filler on, more than brush it on. Use a stiff brush. Swab it on with the grain first, making sure that coverage is complete, although uniformity is of no importance and neatness doesn't necessarily count. Then scrub across the grain. Your objective is to work the filler into the wood grain as deeply and as firmly as possible. You want to pack it in tight so it won't come out when you clean off the surplus.

In a few minutes, the filler will begin to dull over. This means that the liquids are evaporating, leaving mainly solids which are again in a paste form. There is a fairly exact point at which the drying filler is just right for wiping. With practice you'll discover this point. If you wipe too soon, you'll lift filler out of the pores. Wait too long and you'll find it difficult to get the material off the surface.

One good trick is to squeegee the filler cross-grain with a straight, true edge. If you have an old deck of playing cards around the house, they make perfect scrapers. You can use a wide putty knife, edges of wood scraps—anything that rides on the surface, scrapes off surplus filler, and tends to work the material firmly into the pores.

After this, switch to a coarse cloth, excelsior, burlap, or other heavy material. *Work cross-grain only.* Never wipe filler with the grain, or you'll surely wipe it out of the grainwise pores. Wipe as clean as you can. Any filler you leave on the surface obscures the grain and dulls the finish.

Give the filler overnight or longer to dry. If your wiping was thorough, you are now ready to apply the finish. If you can detect any roughness by feel, or if you can see any filler on the surface, get out some extra fine flint paper and a felt-covered sanding block and give the surface a gentle once-over. You want to cut away the unwanted filler, but never sand enough to remove any wood. If you do, you'll open up more wood pores which should be filled.

HOW TO USE LIQUID FILLERS

There is little difference between the liquid filler paint stores sell and the sanding sealer discussed previously. Varnish or lacquer based, they contain a small quantity of solids, usually silicates. These solids fill the pores. Since liquid fillers contain relatively little solid matter, however, they must be used *only on fine-grained woods.* And, in the opinion of many good wood-finishing experts, there is no need to fill such fine-grained species as maple, birch, poplar, basswood, beech, cherry, gum, etc.

Brush on liquid filler about the same as you would a regular finishing coat. There is no point in an extra heavy application, as long as coverage is complete. When the filler is dry, sand carefully. You must get all of the filler off the surface of the wood, leaving it only in the pores, or it will cloud the finish and it may yellow with age. Go at the surplus dried filler with 3/0 or coarser paper, to get quick results. Then switch to 6/0 when you have removed most of it. Be careful not to sand below the original surface, or new pores will open up.